UGLY DUCKLING PRESSE
: dossier :

Sleep's Powers
Originally published as *Puissances du Sommeil,* Editions du Seuil, 1997
Translation © 2008 Jennifer Moxley

ISBN-13: 978-1-933254-42-5

Published by Ugly Duckling Presse, Brooklyn, NY
www.uglyducklingpresse.org

Ugly Duckling Presse titles are distributed to the trade by
Small Press Distribution / SPD
www.spdbooks.org

This publication was partially funded by a grant
from the National Endowment for the Arts.

NATIONAL
ENDOWMENT
FOR THE ARTS
A great nation
deserves great art.

Library of Congress CIP data is available upon request.

SLEEP'S POWERS

Puissances du Sommeil

By Jacqueline Risset

Translated from the French by Jennifer Moxley

TABLE OF CONTENTS

The Enigma	11
The Lecture	13
Another Lecture	15
Speaking of Sleep	17
The Telephone	19
The Most Terrible Tragedy	21
The Sleeping Body in Poems and Paintings	23
Sleep and the Sea	25
Two-Faced	27
Novels	29
Trips	30
The Dangers	31
Cat Nap	32
A Sleep Book	34
Rhythm	36
Laughter	38
Sleep, Death, Life	40
Dream-Programs	41
The Obscure, the Active	44
Drafts	46
The Sleep of an Apple	48
Sleep, Sex, Pleasure	51
Dreams Protect Sleep	54
Sleep Defeats Dreams	55
I Will Never Sleep	56
Presence	58
Hotel Paradiso	59

At the Hospital	60
Sacred Sleep	61
The Blank Voice	63
Real Meaning	64
Mise en Scène	65
Dawn over the Sea	67
Harnessing Sleep	69
Headless and Shy	71
The Sleep-Dream Bloc	73
Sleep with a Cat	74
Sleep with a Baby	75
Sleep, Fatigue, Thought	76
The Seven Sleepers	78
Time	80
Sleep Shines	82
All Must Disappear	83
The Sleep of Zarathustra	85
The Sleep of Odysseus	86
Not of This World	87
The Sleeper Awakened	89
Entrusting Yourself to Sleep	90
Nobody Knows	91
The Ridiculous	92
Can One Love an Insomniac	93
A Strange Piece of Furniture	95
Poets	98
Play	99
Doubts	100
The Other Apartment	102

The East	103
Snow	105
When the Sense Is Sleep	107
Violence	108
Absence	109
Love	111

SLEEP'S POWERS

THE ENIGMA

Sleep defies us. Every day it carries us beyond the threshold of our own understanding: a transition impossible to capture. This enigmatic passage assures us our daily dose of the mysterious and the unknown. We need not bring up other, more complex phenomena; neither need we mention insomnia.

Insomnia, it's true, makes us think of sleep. But at the same time, insomnia's craving for sleep, as its object of desire, assures that it cannot see it. Sleep is the flight of being, the ever elusive, the head on a bed of poppies.

Children are much closer to it, but, contrarily, they refuse it as a state forced on them by adults. Those nights passed reading in bed with a flashlight under the covers. "Knock that off, you'll ruin your eyes." But we know that "ruining our eyes" is just another of those nonsensical prophecies we hear when very young. "If you don't eat your vegetables, you'll … " Slightly comical expressions of the powerless adult. It becomes a game: exasperating their powerlessness we revel in our unexpected ability to immobilize the other …

Seen truthfully, our attempt to understand sleep is also a kind of game, an intractable game of solitaire. Try and capture the moment of falling—out of pure curiosity—and enter its hiding place, uncover the secret: "This time, it won't elude me." With setbacks and failures, but small advances as well—feeling somehow just around the corner from the moment sleep begins—already turned to dreams; the "sleep-dream" bloc rises whole before you, like a continent, like an island whose contours suddenly come into view. I didn't catch you in your emergence, night of sleep, but indirectly you've revealed something else; you've made me see that you are night's inner light, shared with the image inventors, my dreams.

During childhood the repetition of the same dream is both an indication of sleep and the release of other dreams: An evil shrew drops you headfirst into a pond—"evil woman, you threw me in here and I am falling and drowning, but you can't catch me anymore, I'm free now, this is *my* kingdom." The reactive jerk of the body, a jump of fierce denial. Most likely we are made up of such feats, a few invented gestures of puerile self-affirmation, which lead to the powerful feeling (though it is more the freedom *from* feeling than a feeling itself) of being able to overcome a limit. "Though you've put me in this circle, I am more agile than you, and am already outside of it."

The joy of the jump, immediately de-linked from defiance; a simple joy: "Ah! I have the power to jump!" And in doing so not only am I freed from suffocating definitions, but I make contact with the source of all energy. I am not, in effect, nowhere. I am "free."

THE LECTURE

In a vast amphitheatre, late afternoon, first warm days, Paris, summertime.

I see my sentences, my discourse stream, in a state of weightless void and suspension. I calmly continue: citations, comparisons, the question investigated, unpacked.

I overlook this silent human landscape; then all of a sudden I see, while speaking, that here and there several heads are drifting: in the front to the left, farther back to the right. One, very close, falling backward onto the chair's headrest; another, bobbing, bowing forward onto a chest …

With hesitation and a certain amusement I continue. What should I do? Calmly persevere to the end, or gently introduce, without warning, a shocking remark to wake them up—a frivolous anecdote perhaps, or a violent one, something to tear them from their peaceful torpor? I imagine a collective laugh in their sleep, or the smile of angelic infants—and what if I mentioned pacifiers? What would be the equivalent of a pacifier to these—in some cases quite old—sleeping, perhaps even dreaming faces? I try and guess which words or ideas, once they've left my mouth, might continue on as dreams in their heads. A single dream—how nice to imagine it—a dream that could resolve the enigma my talk is attempting to explore, and yet remain true to its own trajectory. How would one extract dreams? For my position behind this lectern, towering over the amphitheatre, it would seem I would need some kind of hook …

At present a few straighten up and rejoin us with a quick start, giving off, with their focus and doubly serious expressions, the semblance of unbroken attentiveness. Those who continue sleeping, slumped in their chairs, wear a completely open expression—the exaggeratedly open expression of the blind, like that of Borges a few years back at a ceremony, *honoris causa,* that took place at the University of Rome. Extremely white taut face. Dressed, like everyone else, in a ceremonial gown, a mortarboard on his head. But, like an animal from a fable, or a cat with a saucepan tied to its tail, he was blind to the laurels being placed on him: tense expression, quasi-ecstatic, lacking any rapport with this academic circumstance, the hat askew on the crown of his head. Through these radical means he managed to evade the heavily consecrated praise.

How strange it feels to speak to these absent people. Perhaps it is always like this—less obvious, but like this. What are we doing when we give a lecture? To whom are we speaking?

Sleep is a kidnapper, or so this and similar episodes would make it seem. It is violence personified: "You have been warned, sleep says, I'll recapture you—resistance is futile—you're mine."

ANOTHER LECTURE

This anecdote concerns my mother who, in her important role as the wife of the organizer, sits in the front row of the large auditorium. Elegantly dressed, often wearing a wide-brimmed black or pink straw hat. We, her children, also attended the lectures. Some interested us—some were simply time away from home, others an occasion for hearing delightful new words and checking out the strange, sometimes comical, characters in the audience and on the stage.

My mother loved attending them. She was passionate about some of the topics, others less so. In either case she always fell asleep. Running around and working from the moment she got up, diligently directing both the main house and the host college, in the evenings, whether at home or out, she would be assailed by waves of abrupt, irrepressible sleep. Sitting with us at the table after the dinner plates had been cleared, as we played or colored—she would draw our portraits—while still upright she would suddenly close her eyes; sometimes she would speak. One night, in the garbled tone of the Delphic oracle, she uttered this mysterious sentence: "Tomorrow we will bring supports to your school." We, thinking that she had heard during the day, in her role as director of a public institution, that a set of parallel bars, or some other exciting playground equipment, was soon to be delivered to our elementary school (at the time our school had nothing of this sort) asked her: "Oh yes mom, what for?" With her eyes still closed she sluggishly replied: "To support evil people."

From thenceforth this phrase became a family legend, though she did not like having it repeated back to her too often. Living totally spontaneously, like a child, denying herself leisure or the permission to stop, never thinking of her own needs, she experienced light-hearted teasing as a withdrawal of affection and it made her very morose. Subsequently she defended herself against our attempts to pull from her sleeping self, with cleverly asked questions, more strange and illuminating sentences. She would continue to sleep, but always with a slight smile, as if she was onto our hijinks.

During lectures it was our job to try and prevent her from falling asleep too obviously—we were supposed to say her name, or, if necessary, pinch her arm; but our efforts were ineffective. Minutes later her hat would begin its gracious plunge, like a large bird drifting on the wind. Everyone in the room could see it, even the lecturer was thrown off topic—or so it seemed to us. And then, the moment we stopped trying to rouse her, the large brim and the head beneath it would suddenly lift, and out from under her wingèd cover she would flash the speaker a dazzling and approving smile. Reassured, he would continue his lecture, until the inevitable moment, not long in coming, when, despite our attempts to keep her awake, the hat would go plunging down again, this time for an even longer siesta.

And yet we children, while taking our duty to prevent these inappropriate lapses very seriously, felt curiously contented by them, as if they vindicated us: We were already overcome by social obligations (lectures were emblematic) and thus felt allied to this asocial behavior, which brought them to their knees. This elementary refusal of the entire adult comedy was a stronger force, and yet it was accepted. The hat, in addition to having the charm of a mask or a carnival costume, was in some ways a symbol of this comedy. And it too was carried off ... sleep, even adult sleep—if feminine—was ours; as a figure of childhood it belonged to us.

SPEAKING OF SLEEP

Speaking of sleep is like speaking of dreams from the outside, from their place of origin. Sleep is the loam of dreams, the material in which they grow. But it is also something more: something hidden, made obscure by the accumulation of images—a sort of grand dream which, because of its intense and manifold nature, is undecipherable. Compared to sleep, dreams offer us a free, easy, almost anodyne, show. Sleep abides from the start in the interior tissue out of which we are formed. Moments of astonishment, precious passages filled with rapid, disconnected symbols—light birds like late evening swallows—a single swallow still squawking overhead, halfway to sleep.

It is difficult to speak of sleep because it appropriates everything that draws near it. In the case of dreams, they will win, hiding sleep in their pocket. But everything else, locales (beds, bedrooms, etc.), surrounding objects (those that we bring, or those brought to mind when we get there), sleep invades, inhabits, and transforms. This is how I felt when in bed at the Grand Hotel by the train station, in the top-floor room with enormous balustrades, surrounded by the sounds of the busy city and the joyous metallic friction and bells of the tramways, where I fell rapidly to sleep, eager to become part of the room, the hotel, the city, all of which soon became emanations of the approaching happy sleep, so distinct from the static, severe, and closed-up feeling of everyday sleep. The next morning I found a chest of toys in the little hall outside my door, perhaps just this once, but it became part of the vision from then on, and appeared each morning, as if the night's crowning gesture. And the elephant I'd seen in the large zoo also showed up in my sleep; I had thought of him the night before, just before falling into total darkness, and he was still there in the morning when I woke up, everything harmoniously arranged around him.

THE TELEPHONE

One day, while talking about something else, he says: "I would like to call you in the evening." "Of course, yes, do." A short time later, in another country, I am awakened by ringing. I reach out in the dark and hear his voice, hurried and intimate. I think to myself, "How can I hide the fact that he's just woken me up?" His voice is tender, joking, a little shy—I'm charmed. As quickly as possibly I attempt to travel the enormous distance from my undoubtedly dream-filled sleep—which is no longer anything but an obscure mass, indistinct, indifferent—but which, in spite of me, puts a catch in my voice. I hear his slow down, become troubled. He talks a little bit more, and then quickly hangs up, before my words, still bound by the ties of sleep, can convey my happiness at his call. I know that the voice he heard did not correspond to the one I wished to project—less still no doubt to, of all my interior voices, the one I use when speaking out loud.

I am, to his awakened state, in a foreign country he can never know. The timidity we feel when waking a lover is linked to our fear of discovering, or verifying, the following: that when compared to the simple quotidian nocturnal discoveries of sleep, our true country of origin, the pull of love is fragile, recent, and less enchanting. Awakened by this beloved voice, I was like Undine ripped from the watery lair of her parents: Though I am moved by my love for the knight, he knows that my home is with them. By his side my step trembles with the desire to reenter the riverbank reeds.

Of course, this isn't true, I am as mortal as he, and his call was pure happiness—not blind, heavy sleep—yet still I failed to dispel his fears. For him, in that moment, I belonged to another place, a place I love more than him, and from which, he thinks, I do not desire rescue. Perhaps the Sabine women were only sleeping—and to wake someone who is sleeping is the emblem of all violent acts.

"If you sleep you prefer someone else, you prefer the gentle arms of Morpheus to mine."

When we wake our lovers we rip them from a divine embrace, we carry them back down to earth, to a settled, mortal love less sweet; we engage in a battle—a losing one, naturally—with a secret contented partner. We unveil the makeshift nature of all earthly love.

THE MOST TERRIBLE TRAGEDY

Where does the cruelty of insomnia—so difficult to withstand, nerves on edge, powerless anxiety—come from? Certainly it is not just from a "lack of rest," but from something much more profound.

According to Cioran it is "the most terrible tragedy that can befall a man," for he who suffers from insomnia will not experience discontinuity, which is the only thing that makes life tolerable: "Much more than to rest, we sleep to forget."

In this way, the programmatic pessimist stops his thought at a fixed point—there is no going beyond. A position which elsewhere lends Cioran's person a singular gaiety, a kind of juvenile insouciance: "From now on let us think of other things, leave aside, just until tomorrow, any attempt to cogitate." And thus with a little task—the task of doing nothing—he rests happily in the tranquility of his pessimistic conclusion, little tormented by the idea of pushing deeper, through doubt, and with no desire to enter the mental landscape of sleep, and in doing so continue the interrogation …

Let us go even deeper, then … to forgetting; a discontinuity, certainly, but not only, and in any case one with a very different meaning. There is also an affirmative side to forgetting (Nietzsche knew of it, not Cioran): the happiness of the moment, the joy, the incomparable energy of birth: specifically born of forgetting. "He who is incapable when facing the threshold of forgetting the past, without fear or vertigo, will never know happiness."

Discontinuity is surprise, transport by repeated pains and

shocks. At the same time it is the joy of the contradiction, of the breeze of another thought arriving on the air without explanation.

Strange to think of thought beginning after carefully closing the windows, with the knowledge that a conclusion has already been reached—a conclusion that feels satisfied (if briefly) with being "different," and feels stronger than the average thought (is there any such thing as an "average" thought?).

And yet it is meaningless to talk about sleep in terms of discontinuity and forgetting. It opens a confused and displacing space into which pocked, slippery, and disquieting thoughts enter, bringing oblivion with them. But, above all, it is there that we seize that microscopic fabric that is the foundation of all our being—a vague material, soft and uninterrupted, a continuity of mental coloring from which, every once in a while, *one* thought or *one* idea detaches. The sensual pleasure of sleep's outskirts is there as well, miming, with irony, with grace, your mental discoveries, both the present and the imminent, opening a path to futures as well … running through the entire fabric, the entire space between thought and feeling, which at the same time is revealed to be one landscape, not two.

THE SLEEPING BODY IN POEMS AND PAINTINGS

Body and face of a sleeping woman: a figure of love, in which everything is gathered up and takes refuge in itself, warmth and silence, regard/disregard.

The words "sleepy," and "sleepyhead": words of love and desire; the sensuality of the poems in which they appear (in Ronsard, and many others). A truce in love's battle: Before she wakes up she is in love; she loves herself; she loves the person who loves her, and who knows ("Darling … ").

The beautiful knowledge of sleep's origins. The body, like an intimate treasure—intimate but very guarded and silent. Time of a caress, unknown and unnoticed, penetrating the skin's wall just to the heart, just to the heart of the dream where it undoubtedly scatters into all sorts of images—light—like golden fishes.

The gaze is the caress that does not awaken. Louis Marin: "*The painter's canvas is a sleeping body.*"

There are many sleeping bodies in Poussin's paintings. *Diana and Acteon,* from his juvenilia: In the forefront of the canvas a woman sleeps, visible to none but the viewer. The viewer is Acteon to this sleeping woman's Diana. This doubling of scenes suspends the action and moves the moment of cruelty—when Acteon's dogs rip him to shreds—to the foreground, into thought, into the gaze like a caress and a meditation.

In *Renaud and Armide* it is the man who sleeps and the woman who looks. And the gaze finds itself pulled into the cloth of this sensual sleep, the sleep of childhood floating around the trappings of the disarmed warrior; in this instant love is born. It is born from the revelation of the other body, the tender nocturnal body that the daytime body (the warrior) undresses.

The relationship between painting and language is renewed: Louis Marin asks, "How can we speak about a sleeping body?" He answers: "By using this enormous body of language which is also, at its deep core, a sleeping body."

Barely emerging from the depths, the great body of language, awakened by our brief gestures, brings us gold, flashes of playful and revelatory light. Revealing of what? Light itself, and revelation.

SLEEP AND THE SEA

Nothing is more down-to-earth, more grounded in appearance, than a sleeping body: a breathing shard of primordial clay. Yet respiration recalls the sea, and the regular motion of the waves.

"At day's end it wasn't just the sea that lived for me in Albertine, but, at times, the drowsiness of the sea as it looked on the beach under a full moon … "

"In that light her sleep became, to a certain degree, the possibility of love … She was hidden, enveloped, returned into her body … her life … exhaling her light breath toward me. I listened to the mysterious murmuring emanation, soft like an ocean zephyr, enchanted like moonlight, that was her sleep."

Sleep, which encloses this being in her body, is moonlight on the sea, interior and exterior both. It will return in adjacent pages in different locales and forms, the way moonlight moves across summer nights creating different sky-scapes. Language imperceptibly changes: "I embarked on the sleep of Albertine." A lightly grazed exchange, encounter.

"Sleep, like the sea, alludes to a very ancient human state, 'Thalassa'—our aquatic ancestors" (Ferenczi). Each night, while asleep, the beings she bore return to her waters—to their place of origin, more distant and profound than the earth.

Like the giant Anteaus, who recovered his strength every time he touched his foot to his mother the Earth, each night we humans place our cheeks on a pillow that is not only "the cheek of our childhood" but the face of our grandmother, the sea. We return to the unknown place from whence we came and that still lights us like the light of the moon, a light of memory that travels the nights, the centuries, the splendors. And we reemerge from her in the morning, almost cleansed of forgetting …

TWO-FACED

Sleep holds dreams inside it like fruit pulp inside the peel; it offers them up, like a fruit, or a thought:

"All will be resolved, she said upon waking / because sleep has made me a gift of thought / and my memory is a succulent fruit / more succulent than the new sun / gently lighting my warm drapes" (Paul Eluard).

And the happiness of waking up, when to do so feels like the sun which "lights the warm drapes," is made up of the sensual numbness of limbs still committed to the warmth of the bed and the primordial torpor; the tissue of images which belong to night, that album we leaf through before throwing ourselves into the new day, before it barges in on us, adds to this feeling as well.

When sleep tries to hold on—to make sense of a dream, or at any cost to change the dream's ending—or when it launches into some incessant mental work, over and over again, like the relentless persistence of a harpsichord insistently playing in the head …

Sleep can also put a stop to things:
"Athena poured sleep over the suitors to stop their plotting so that Telemachus could leave Ithaca free of worry."

Sleep gives rise to thinking and paralyses all thought. It restores strength, is a source of energy and health, the dew of being, and at the same time it is complete powerlessness, the image of death, and our first experience of the "big sleep." And the journey between the one and the other, when made via an innocent afternoon nap—foundering little by little just until you feel grabbed, prevented from returning—a kind of terror, therefore, before the difficult victory of waking up, just as soon forgotten …

NOVELS

In novels the heroes are wide awake—they have things to do, they must shape their characters and find victory ... but on occasion they need help waking up. Sometimes they are awakened by gods, like Odysseus, who suddenly sees Athena next to his bed, larger than a mortal woman, so that he knows who she is, even in this semi-lucid moment.

Sometimes we see their dreams, or one of them recounts a dream. But for a hero to be sleepy, or tired, is uncommon enough. You see it in Kafka and Bataille, but few others.

There is Proust, of course. *The Search for Lost Time* bathes in dreams. They emerge from the text like Venus from the sea, and just as Venus never severs her connection to the sea—to foam, sperm, and charms—Proust's text never loses sight of its origin. Dreams, but not only, dreams and sleep, sleep and waking. It is there, he says, that we find, over and over again, not only time, but truth itself, which lives nowhere else. ("One cannot describe men's lives accurately without understanding their sleep, where those lives are shaped, night after night, like a peninsula carved by the sea.")

A happy disdain for philosophies: "Through sleep, my dear fellows, I surpass you, since it is unclear whether I am sleeping or living, sleeping or thinking."

And what is thought if not letting the forms exit the shadows that gave birth to them? A passive and difficult labor achieved in opposition to the conscious will.

TRIPS

Mysterious childhood train trips: I am often ill. Abrupt feverish naps interrupt the passing countryside. But the source of my feeling of mystery, very strong and very specific, is a red veil covering my face—perhaps it happened only this once, but my memory of it is such that I am unsure if it was on a very long trip, where we changed trains often, with me in someone's arms being carried through the crowd, or—a less likely hypothesis—on several trips, on all the trips of my childhood. It was probably related to an illness—I was frequently ill—perhaps the measles (both my fever and my red spots shielded by the veil?). I can still feel the slight pressure of it on my skin, and I can see the train station and the unified movement of the crowd distanced and embellished through this singular shade. It is as though I have been pushed down into sleep, wrapped in a veil of sleep itself. Existing in this luminous shadow I am both very near and very far from everything.

On long train trips often someone would hang a little hammock for me from the baggage rack of our compartment. I would jubilantly assist in its difficult installation. And then, more pleasure. While the same regular movement was rocking me as the other passengers, I was also apart from them, higher up, in the jungle. I was Tarzan—a bit immobilized, squished by the ropes of the hammock, smothered with covers and p-jays, but Tarzan nonetheless. Though lions and other big cats I might fight off were a bit scarce, I knew that they could appear at any moment, fierce ones. A little blue night-light (that bothered the adults—they would never let me have one at home) which shone throughout the night here, would help me hunt them when the time came. I fell asleep, protected, in my creeping vines.

THE DANGERS

The dangers of sleep: the menacing animals it allows to quickly take over the entire bedroom: large yellow-eyed cats, pillow clamping monkeys. The distinction between states is still fuzzy, and it is not altogether clear that these forms, lingering a few moments after waking up, are dreams. They are the products of sleep and of the bed, and are therefore a good reason to refuse to go to bed at night when other people in the house are still up. Far removed from such dangers, they calmly lead you to the claws of these evil creatures waiting in the dark.

Later, having learned the word "nightmare," I see something hidden, it makes a pool appear, a stain of cold black water, like rain deposits on the street or a puddle in a squalid rural area—chaotic poultry yard, menacing geese, biting ducks.

Just before falling asleep, like a regular ritual, every night, four or five years old: The first thing I see is a pool, as a matter of fact. Round and black, on a vast flat landscape. On its bank stands a woman, a fairly plump housewife, wearing a ponytail and a long grey dress or apron. Expressionless and immobile, she holds a very small child upright at the end of her extended arms. Her hands are resting under the child's armpits, and then suddenly, as if on cue, they symmetrically move apart. I feel them separate—and then black water encompasses my little forehead. It's the same every night. I fall into the abyss of sleep, into the nightmare pool.

CAT NAP

In French the word "sommeil" (sleep) comes from "petit somme"—in Latin *somniculus*—a word that falls apart in the mouth. Here etymology shows us the path of destruction in language, once a strong and resistant edifice: the word becomes something to eat, to suck; gone is the serious issue of pronunciation or the differentiation between letters and sounds.

The word "soleil" (sun—*soliculus*) also derives from the diminutive. Therefore, via late Latin, from a couple of attenuated vocables, the language inherits both a name for the king of stars, and for the vast amount of time that flees it, and to which we aspire—the two together making up, more or less, the totality of our lives.

Through the rhyme they share, a perfect rhyme, *soleil* and *sommeil* answer each other with a Cratylus-like countersound similar to the one which arises, as Mallarmé noted, when reversing the words "nuit" and "jour" (*nuit* a "luminescent" word, while *jour* "darkens a bit").

Sommeil rhymes with both *éveil* (awakening) and with the source of all light, the sun star—the exclusion and fleeing from which is the first act of anyone who lies down for a nap: "To sleep, we retire to an obscure place; we stretch out on a surface horizontal and soft … "

In what measure, for a French speaker, is sleep colored by the proximity of sun? The English word *sleep* has but a single slither, lightly crawling: the sleep of the *serpent*. One becomes a snake when sleeping: body stretched out, a bit dissolved, which certainly facilitates our access to dreams, and makes waking up more difficult: liquefaction approaches, watch out, SLEEP!

The Italian *sonno* returns to the root conjugations of sleep and dream, *somnus* and *somnium* (for which Spanish has only one word: *sueño*). But instead of giving off a sense of the possibility of dreams and their fireworks, the word *sonno* is immobilized by its *o*: heavy sleep, thick, announcing the finale. Whereas the god *Hypnos* pours his libation over us whenever he feels like it … let's not over-think it.

A SLEEP BOOK

We can dream of books that emerge from sleep as though stepping out of a warm bath, its essence clings to them, its drops of water, its rosy warmth. But few writers, indeed few characters, have the courage to give in so completely to a sleep that enlivens and unites our cares with fragile leaves of grass, like a single sentence gliding insensibly over a soft horizontal surface. This is sleep and dreams together, with neither dominating; sleep and dreams as seen through literature and literature as seen as the full and effusive use of language, in this case French—a language of water, both slippery and transparent, wonderful and soporific. In *Le Sentiment géographique* (*The Geographic Feeling*), Michel Chaillou peruses both the Loire valley and the first few pages of the six thousand that make up Honoré d'Urfé's pastoral novel *Astrea*, by connecting and melting their components together like sleep and dreams.

His account restores to the grass, to the water, to the language, to the bodies of those who live in it (pages of half-asleep shepherds) and read it (we swim while sleeping, and gather plants) a kind of plenitude, and living meaning. A complicity between the writer, the reader, the sleeper, and the dreamer. And also landscapes as the culminating visions of many successive eras. Water-rich valleys like landscape mirrors in which you can still see, wavering, the dainty profile of a few silhouettes resembling a grand Louis XIII-style feathered hat, trimmed with fur and buckles.

The jolts of sleep are also represented in this stream. It carries us along, gently rocking and slipping—but it is also troubled, with sudden interruptions—and sudden downfalls. Celadon and Astrea are also like a verdant landscape. Words and clods of earth and skin, great soft naked and gorgeous bodies in myriad pastoral concerts where what we love awakens—Astrea and Celadon melt into this seventeen-century French literary countryside, in an uninterrupted line they lead straight toward us, toward the westward hills of Forez, toward the setting sun.

RHYTHM

The rhythm of the sentence holds the secret to the rhythm of this so-called "novel"—a machine to capture the imaginary and all that flowers forth from the unconscious. In other words, to enter into the secretly rhythmic and slippery time of sleep which dreams can emerge from at any moment.

Thus the door in the back left corner of the large hotel room where I fell asleep this evening is suddenly pierced open. I enter the room and walk across it. I see a young woman with a pale and serious face and, next to her, a little behind, a watchful young man, who appears to be in a hurry. They are both moving toward the back of the room, where a tiny door that I haven't yet seen stands open. I understand that she is taking them to their room. I ask what they are doing. Her response is incomprehensible, and he intervenes with a steadfast look: "Setting sail." I realize that they are trying to leave without paying their hotel bill. Then, with a slight English accent, the young woman addresses me, calling me by name. It suddenly occurs to me that they aren't just deadbeats—hotel thieves? terrorists?—their level of determination is disproportionate to simply wanting to skip out on a bill. She then explains something to me about how they need extra time in order to put some money in the bank, a story so innocent I wonder why she can't just explain it to the hotel porter. I say nothing, having already decided I will help them—after all, in this provincial hotel where nothing much happens, this scenario is fairly interesting. I don't even really know why I'm here, or what I'm waiting for, except vaguely that I'm slated to leave on a voyage in a few days, to board a ship. But where is the sea?

Sleep opens a door to mysterious, almost mute characters—and it should be rendered in sentences which imitate its quasi-imperceptible movement, its capacity—fluvial, certainly—to annul, without stopping and slipping, or being detected, without letting the materials entering the stream know what it is they're entering, lest they change their minds at the last minute, or alarming the inhabitants and stopping the train, or causing the pen to lift pensively off the paper, sentences which at the same time establish a kind of litany, a rocking back and forth, with no alternation between strong and gentle beats—then there is no need to fall deeper into sleep, just keep accessing this movement, which carries you through its continuous and very tenuous opening, which can, from moment to moment, easily be lost. It is an empty rhythm and the French language, especially that of the seventeenth-century, the language of Racine and of *Astrea*, flows in it, a transparent water which runs along, lettings things enter the flood in such a way that they don't seem strange or unfamiliar; this is also the foundation of Verlaine's language, and that of Rimbaud and Apollinaire, but most of all it is the power, the gentleness, of Swann's little *phrase*.

LAUGHTER

This book of water and dreams (Urfé's *Astrea*) finishes by touching on, in a discussion about literature, the most dangerous, fear-inducing, and irreversible aspect of sleep—the fear of not waking up—but here it is reversed to become the fear of waking up, though we sense that they are the same thing. By following its course through writing, sleep bumps up against the unknown—as when a boat approaches very close to the reeds of the river and causes the animals hiding there to scatter. It creates a beautiful reversal, for example: When examined closely, *Astrea*, a nearly forgotten novel vaguely perceived as the opposite of all writing we might call "modern" (which is similar to dreams), shakes the foundation and dissolves the boundaries. The fascination this holds lies in the overlooked relationship imposed by the words between the countryside of the Loire, the words and the sentences of this famous, yet unread, novel, and the rhythm with which sleep dominates someone—the reader …

It is clear that reading, like sleep, is a wager, so similar to sleep its meaning is doubled, and slightly comic as well. Apart from the "big sleep," nothing is serious about sleep, since sleep is itself a parody of the "big sleep." When asleep we live with the servants of comedy, there where tragedy can never fully take hold. But sleep connects to dreams, and through them everything gets back in (everything serious and symbolic). Comic (parodic) sleep is called "deep dreamless sleep." But it has now been shown to be precisely during our very deepest sleep, when we are as immobile as a stone and our motor functions have ceased, that dreaming begins and brain activity is most intense—the time of paradoxical sleep—but perhaps all sleep is paradoxical.

A proposal on how to read: Suspend judgment, let the words appear in your mind as laughter sometimes does, when your guard is down, for example, and you're still a little drowsy. At the same time let the (liquid) countryside of the Loire and the mental (amorous) universe of the pastoral shepherds, imprisoned by the sleepy rhythm of the long sentences and water of Honoré d'Urfé's transparent French, slip without resistance into your consciousness as the reader, and into other books as well.

SLEEP, DEATH, LIFE

Night is a place of death, sleep is its sign: Sleep makes the precariousness of breathing—beneath its comforting wave-like motion—evident, as well as the incessant grief that pervades all life. Nietzsche: "Underneath the respiration of the sleeper, his disquieting rhythm, a perpetually renewed grief seems to sound a melody—we don't hear it, but when the breast of the sleeper rises, we sense that the heart is being constrained, and when the breathing diminishes, almost expiring in a deathlike sleep, we say to ourselves: 'Rest a while, poor tormented spirit!' We wish for all the living—for all are subject to the same oppression—eternal rest; night invites death."

At night, facing sleep, the man who loves daytime and light must be reconciled to darkness and death. Sleep already knows this angle, though the sleeper does not. We cannot see ourselves sleep, anymore than a body, once consciousness is gone from it, can see its own death.

The sleeping body: an object denied self-control offered up as an erotic fantasy, or a comic object, like the vicar who, in the meticulous pages of Michel Jouvet's *Chateau des songes*, drowses under the watchful eye of the amateur naturalist Hughes de la Scève, a Franche-comté gentleman who had observed the instantaneous relaxing of a rabbit's neck muscles when it fell into a brutal post-coital sleep. Deep sleep, the sleep of dreams, where the body of the dreamer is at the attacker's mercy.

DREAM-PROGRAMS

In order to justify the defenseless position sleep puts us in we must assume, along with the research scientists, that it fulfills a unique function: According to Michel Jouvet this function is to assure our individuation, which might otherwise prove insufficient or be lost.

How attractive to come up with a hypothesis which overturns our vision of sleep as a theatrical repetition of death. No, the dreamer-sleeper (at the heart of sleep, in its profound center, inaccessible, insensible) is not prey to the grief that presses heavily on all the living, neither is he simply resting; he is busy inventing his life.

This is not about prophetic dreams, which are no better than those thematically juvenile "dream dictionaries," but about "dream-programs," where our future behavior is elaborated—and, more exciting still, about freedom—insofar as the dream allows us to know in advance, internally, a reality we might soon encounter. Dreams don't leave me prey to death, to the death I am already living, participating in, from this day forward until the big sleep. They do just the opposite; by giving myself completely over to sleep I discover the catch point to the directives that will go into forming my life. Merlin the magician speaks to me—the sage, Chiron the centaur, knows where to take me, how to give me the empowering vision …

Memory of a summer dream—I don't know if it merits the category of an individuating "dream-program," but for me it had the weight of an experience lived *in advance*, not prophetic, but divinatory and initiative. It was a sexual dream I had while still a pre-teen. At the time, I had a rather dim and totally bookish concept of sex. The dream, quite different from what I had read in books, was precise and, as I would later verify, quite exact. I remember my partner—it was a friend of my brother's, slightly younger than me, who had been gently courting me in waking life, as had some others boys from the same group; I liked him fairly well, but not particularly; all of these boys were a bit too young, and therefore of limited interest to me. On this point I admire the intelligence of the dream, which, in choosing this boy instead of one of the others, some of whom, at the time, I liked better, made certain that the experience didn't take on the much more familiar form or name of "love." Not being in love, I followed the act in my dream with interest, but without overwhelming emotion, scrutinizing the unfolding of gestures on my body, the growing intensity, the denouement: Consequently there was more understanding, a closeness, a justness ... and a feeling, satisfying to him as well, of the abstract generality typical of lessons. My partner, whom I recognized and knew in daily life, did not take on that nimbus or aura of tender intimidation that attaches itself the morning after to those who, though we feel indifferent about them, we have tenderly dreamt about the night before, only a sort of bemused and secret recognition from which he did not benefit. Not, that is, until a few years later, when the two of us entered into an extended and dreamy flirtation, filled with kisses, garden rendezvous, and inflamed love letters, but which never led to the act, to which he had, after all, introduced me.

I remember how after this dream I scrutinized my other dreams in an entirely new way; and that many were the times, though never again in such a radical and troubling fashion, that I recognized, in connection to other types of experience, this same anticipatory power that dreams can sometimes have over existence.

It does not seem to me that this explanation—if indeed it is an explanation—weakens the Freudian reading. The expression of a specific desire can also be that of a "general" desire—a desire to know desire—and if an analytical reading renders certain elements passé, condensation and displacement in the masculine figure, for example, or the realization and prolonging of old sensations in characterizing the "primal scene," all this can be reconciled, I believe, with the anticipation of experience.

"The true paradises are those we have lost," the new is made up from parts of the old, which suddenly revive, reigniting …

THE OBSCURE, THE ACTIVE

Sleep conceals a mystery—a mystery born when we abandon our reason. Reason finds pleasure in its own defeat, pleasure and a new form of reason filled with new lands to explore and the knowledge of another life, which is also reason's child.

The most mysterious point of sleep is not the interior of the immanent dream, with its profusion of given images—an unexpected, unforeseeable gift—but rather the complete absence of images, and the powerful gesture (giant soft hand) that erases the slate of day.

Thus our being plunges wholly into obscurity. And this thin trace of light that allows us to perceive the obscurity—a coquetry (of the obscure)—which refuses to be caught as it grabs you, taking over and replacing everything ...

To interrogate sleep, in the simple sense of scrutinizing it in an attempt to extract its secret, we must take the exact opposite stance of all other analytical methods. Torpor is generally forbidden in the study. Here, by contrast, it is privileged: when studying sleep it is permissible, even necessary, to fall asleep, sleep must be both the object and subject of the work. Here the sign on the door of Saint-Pol Roux: "Poet at work: dreaming" becomes: "Hard at work: sleeping."

The paradox of paradoxical sleep is this: mental activity peaks when we sleep most deeply, the moment our motor functions stop working and it becomes most difficult to wake us. Eyes move, neurons circulate, *it* thinks: dreams begin.

This is how sleep prolongs dreams. But where does the flesh

of the other begin? Is the heart of sleep therefore this imaginative, prophetic, proliferation?

DRAFTS

The most recent Pléiade edition of *The Search for Lost Time* was enriched by previously unpublished paragraphs inserted into the text or the margins, surprise packages for the reader, like fine chocolates—the tasting of unexpected delicacies, little Proustian presents.

In the rough draft of the first few pages there were several metaphors that were struck from the definitive text. The narrator speaks of himself as the most silent point in the silence of the room where he is sleeping. He compares this idea to that of an apple asleep in the back of an armoire—of an apple and also (in several sketches) a jam jar—this is the height and heart of the secret gift to the reader.

What comes into play with these two abandoned figures is Proust's most profound resource as a writer: his power to identify, not only with the interior life of other people, but to coincide, psychologically in a way, with *all* possible forms of being, including the non-human.

This sort of identification, essential to literature, is also a characteristic of sleep, and of the elemental mechanism which the sleeper himself verifies in the moment when while reading a book he realizes he is asleep, before entering into dreams for good: "I had the impression that I was the things that the book talked about: a church, a quartet, the rivalry between Francois I and Charles Quint ... "

Characteristic of sleep, but indispensable to writing. And it is precisely in order to more accurately describe the nature of sleep that, in the drafts, where Proust endlessly elaborates the start of his long book, he uses such unusual metaphors, "low" ones, which evoke the traces of his childhood identifications.

Whether speaking of the "novel" or "poetry," "characters" or "metaphors," it is the same process, the same means, the same ability to glide into the skin of another, whether this other be a church, a quartet, or the rivalry between historical figures. An ability, in Proust's case, without limits: the heart of the creative process, but difficult to get at ... The apple and the jam jar are identified with the sleeper, that is to say with sleep itself.

THE SLEEP OF AN APPLE

Draft I, sixteenth fragment: "I used to know, like everyone else, the sweetness of waking up in the middle of the night, of for a moment tasting the darkness, the silence, a dull creaking, like the sound that might be made in the back of an armoire by an apple brought for an instant to a weak consciousness of its situation ... "

A tranquil reversal: The apple is not tasted—as, for example, in humanity's mythic history. Rather it is the apple that *tastes*—it tastes the darkness, the silence, like a true Marcel.

The second draft, second fragment, goes against the familiar "For a long time ... ": "Until around the age of twenty, I slept nights," and follows with a definition of sleep as "participation": "A sort of participation in the darkness of the room, in the unconscious life of its compartments and furniture, such was my sleep. I only stopped it to get to know that little part of every sleep that is enlightened, and watches the remainder fall to sleep, turn off ... After having surprised the eddies of the darkness and the creaking wainscoting, I fell back asleep very quickly, a little like an apple, or a jam jar brought to consciousness for an instant and, having confirmed that it is blackest night in the armoire, and having heard the wood working, has nothing more pressing to do than to return to the delicious unconsciousness of the shelf on which it is sitting, and of the other jam jars in the darkness."

This time the apple and jam jar are placed side by side in the armoire drawer. The "jam jar," an object even less like the sleeper than the apple, is therefore better suited to reinforce, at a whole other level, the writer's intuitions about the nature of sleep and night. More distant, less sensate, but also more childlike, the jam jar belongs to the world of *Dame Tartine* and to images from fairytales; it is not far from *Francois le Champi* nor from the colorful Combray desserts—strawberries crushed into cream, turning pink, like sun-drenched skin or a blush, an extraordinary metamorphoses. Awakened for an instant into consciousness, the jam jar perceives, like the sleeper and the apple, the "eddies of the darkness." It hears the wood at work. All is right with the world: Night reigns in the armoire over the jams, the workers (of wood) are at work. And the expression *"having nothing more pressing,"* applied to the fruit and the jar, implies a familiar rather than disturbing haste. A expression of *Heimlich*—of a longing to feel "at home," in one's own space and house, in other words, asleep.

"Unconsciousness is delicious": an eminently Proustian maxim. It completes this other, also central: "Feeling and thinking, such sad things." The experience of suffering instigates a flight from feeling. But it concerns utopia, an aspiration quickly demented by the real: No more than with marriages, there are delicious insensibilities. Here the figure is invented by the insomniac, by the invalid, by the too-sensitive Marcel. The "I" who "for a long time" went to bed early is neither happy nor "at home" except as part of the vast sleep world where he can disappear.

And the first pages of the book are not just a description of the "edges of sleep and sleeplessness"—as Elstir, a bit further on, will use painting to explore the limits of earth and sea—but like a visitation from the interior territories of night: "A sort of participation in the darkness of the room, in the unconscious life of its compartments and furniture, such was my sleep."

The word "unconscious" flowers, and this notion of "participation" is a notion which, during the same era, anthropologists were attempting to define, and would eventually call "magical thought," and later still "wild thought." *The Search for Lost Time*, having barely begun, definitively leaves behind the habitual categories of thought; this is the function of sleep, for it is our nearest quotidian experience of a place where the dominance of the individual is no longer in circulation—an apple, a jar in an armoire, prove just as adequate. Sleep, great maternal belly of ocean eddies, retrieves the lost particles—risen for an instant to consciousness—which have imprudently attempted to go off on their own …

SLEEP, SEX, PLEASURE

The description of happily falling asleep during childhood and adolescence turns very quickly in draft III to sexual awakening in sleep (which appears also, albeit in a summary fashion, in the definitive version in the first pages of *Swann's Way*: "a woman born from an uncomfortable position of my thigh") and is continued, on the next page, with the discovery of masturbation—lines that will later be consecrated in the text we all know but placed farther on and considerably abridged in comparison with this draft. Indeed, these sensations, first publicly said to "never return except in dreams," are here presented as the flowerings of sleep, while in the final version they will, throughout the book, be attached uniquely to childhood, Combray, and the water closet that smelled of orris root:

"I didn't dare speak of these sensations, which returned sometimes in my sleep, it was as if they had appeared, almost poetically, detached from the entirety of my present life, white like water flowers whose roots never touch the ground."

In order to make the description "poetic," or "almost poetic," he resorts to the gracious image of the "water fountain in the park at Saint-Cloud":

"Finally, an opal jet arose, by successive waves, as if, in the moment it darted up, it was the jet of water in Saint-Cloud which we recognized—because the incessant flow of its waters was individuated by the gracious outline of its resistant curve—in the portrait that was left to Hubert Robert ... "

And sexual pleasure, having opened the *Search*, is immediately linked through his young experimentation to Evil—in a "poetic" way again, but clearly:

"On the leaf I had only left a natural silvery trace, like that made by a spider's web or a snail. But on the branch it seemed to me like the forbidden fruit of the tree of evil." Through the sudden amplification of the universe created by the consciousness of pleasure, childhood masturbation presents itself as the first "madeleine" (the first of these experiments with limits which distance all threats, even the reality of "death itself": "I had stopped thinking of myself as mediocre, contingent, mortal"). The draft is revelatory:

"My thought, exalted by the pleasure, sensed that it was more vast, more powerful than the universe I perceived in the distance through my window, and was of the immensity and eternity which I usually thought about with sadness because I was nothing but an ephemeral part of it. In this moment I sensed that my spirit would go even farther than the clouds accumulating over the forest, even farther than the extremity of these things and was not completely filled with them, a small margin was left over. I sensed the powerful gaze of my pupils holding, like simple reflections without reality, the two beautiful curved hills that rose like breasts from the two sides of the river. All of this rested on me, I was more than it, I could not die."

"Assignment: analyze what is profound about pleasure." This little sentence from the *Carnet de 1908* (a moment of global intuition concerning the future book) becomes clearer after reading the above lines.

My point is not, of course, to reduce all Proustian epiphanies to the mechanism of childhood masturbation, in other words, to the surprise of sexual revelation, in which case the entire writing of the book would be nothing from then on but the search for approximations, or more presentable equivalents of it. It is, one could say, just the opposite, insofar as the characteristic gesture here is that of vigorously returning to first signs. It is not sex that sustains, controls, or resolves the other plans. Though there is no doubt that it shows up—in this third sketch—as the first among the "instants" that will punctuate the entire oeuvre. But this episode is, in itself, only an approximation of a much greater truth to which it finally doesn't hold the key. Can we mention sublimation? The other epiphanies will be, in appearance at least, nonsexual, or asexual, which does not prevent the metamorphosis from taking place. The ordinary schema is not sufficient. It is necessary to go beyond.

DREAMS PROTECT SLEEP

I am in our vacation house, in the summertime. It feels cool outside, so it's probably early September. My room looks out onto the countryside, the pines and olive trees. I think: In a few days I will need a blanket, my sleeping body needs a little weight on it, the sheet by itself is giving me a slightly uncomfortable feeling of absence and transparency.

This is the point at which I wake up in my urban apartment; I'm a bit chilly. It is autumn and I do need a blanket, but right now, not in a few days. I recall the dream—the situation is identical, the same brisk air; I get up in the dark and look for a throw in the armoire.

My dream tried to prevent the necessity of waking up and getting out of bed. I awoke in spite of it. At the same time it gave me advice; my state is neither confused nor hesitant. I went straight to the armoire, and now I'm writing on sleep and dreams, something I have been trying to do, without being able to, for several days.

Near the end of sleep, toward morning, the dream is fearful. It is fearful because it will die. It dies at the end of sleep, at the moment when a solution, a complete solution, is imminent: love finally realized, the beautiful countryside from childhood reached, someone lost found, an entire series of never-thought-of situations that will become accessible, thanks to this still mysterious but very simple resource. Solutions which seem more real than the real— I was close to waking up, the goal was now to put it off a few more instants in an effort to understand the mechanism once and for all ...

Too late, the fear is too great, it destroys the house where everything is unfolding and the infiltration begins: the outside, the morning, the day, noise.

SLEEP DEFEATS DREAMS

Dreams, as they are used, for example, in analysis, take an interest in our interests, giving us a gentle hand. Since at the moment I am always thinking about sleep, from time to time my dreams send me a dream about sleep.

I am at F.'s house: we are tranquilly talking about this, that, and the other. A time simple and clear; what is thought of as a conversation perhaps; gentle and suspended, in a regular and regulated exchange, harmonious. It occurs to me that it may be time to think about music, time for F. to take up his instrument and—this part is somewhat vague—for me either to read a poem or play the piano part. At the same moment I realize the impossibility of this because, a few months previously, F.'s instrument was stolen. He, for his part, has had the same idea at the same moment, and has discovered the same problem.

I am then overwhelmed by the thought, which I share with him, that he must quickly buy another cello. At that moment his companion walks through the room, absorbed and distracted. I tell her my feelings about the purchase. She doesn't respond. F. informs her that she is tired and should perhaps go to sleep. I look at her and realize that she is incomplete, in pieces, because my eyes are closing—I no longer see anything—I fall asleep.

In the very same moment—I experience them as simultaneous—I wake up while retrieving, like a fish in a net, this dream about sleep: sleep entering the dream with a certain irony. Sleep is the father of dreams, yes, but the dream is done for should sleep show up.

I WILL NEVER SLEEP

First memories, childhood nights, beginning with the impossibility or hatred of sleep, and with nightmares.
    Fear of sleep. Fear of the dark.

Obligatory sleep—like one of those laws born of adult caprice, a kind of authoritarian fantasy. I do not believe one whit in the necessity, in the "good" that, according to them, sleep will do me. How is it possible to believe in the good of something that excites such terrifying images, that necessitates an abominable dark in my room and interrupts far more interesting occupations, like playing or reading in bed?

I don't believe in the necessity of sleep, any more than I do, and for the same reasons, in that of meals. Sleep and food from time to time—when one voluntarily chooses them—could be, certainly, pleasurable. I think about the kind of unbridled idealism propagated by this form of education: I obey your senseless laws to please you. The kingdom of necessity belongs to you. For me I only know and love infinite liberty, peopled with pleasures that arise and then fade freely away. My life, unlike yours, is inventing itself, starting over in every moment. As one who is continually being reborn how am I to take your monotonous habits seriously?
    —If I finally give in, perhaps it's the draw of the sensual pleasure caused by a fear of the dark, or by the anticipation of being punished for reading under the covers?
    —No

More likely it's a kind of contract. If I do what you tell me you'll leave me alone, so I can vanish into my dream, physically present, but mentally attending to the many little things that escape you, awaiting the sparks of a few silent astonishments. Sleep? It is part of the family comedy preceded by the fatidic parental "calm down!"—a scolding which provokes the opposite reaction. As soon as the words are spoken, I am thrown into a devilishly gleeful frenzy: Look, I'll show you calm, I'll show you sleep, look dad, see how far I am, see how you have no power over me, see how I defy your command: I will never, ever fall asleep!

PRESENCE

A memory of sleep's vast plain of immobile night suddenly ripped apart by the abrupt and terrifying shock of a nightmare. Refuge in the bed of my little brother.

Or the first time it proves impossible: I can't fall asleep because of a toothache. There is someone close by, at the edge of the bed, my mother. She is there, but separate. The pain, which is much closer to me, puts an insurmountable distance between us. Stupor: So, are we alone? always?

On the other hand I remember moments of her being completely present while sleep approached; she sits on the other side of my room, veiled in light, sewing, or writing. In this circumstance falling asleep had a different meaning. It was no longer about leaving behind, or having already left behind, the bright, joyful, inhabited world, and diving into that semi-darkness which spreads until there is no way out. No, in this case it felt like I was part of this attentive scene, the lamp, her living silence, as though I was both continuing with my day and falling asleep—without being watched too closely. But someone has taken charge of the perpetuation of things; it's okay to be absent. And sleep becomes similar—parallel and similar—to the studious activity in its margins. From that moment on you can go to sleep with confidence and seriousness. You are raised up, supported by this presence continuing on in the dim light. Thus calmed, you consent to the time and place.

HOTEL PARADISO

Night at the Hotel Paradiso, in the center of town, near the marketplace and the embassy. Both the name and place please me, and the rooms are adequately comfortable. I will spend several nights here, waiting to be moved into the larger room with a fireplace where I live when I come here for longer stays.

I wake up in the middle of the night and go into the hallway looking for the bathroom. A long hallway, darkness, a door. I push open the door and find myself still in total darkness. I feel as if I have entered a vast room, with some sort of curtain directly in front of me. I am immediately struck by the sound—a noise like no other, like breathing, but immense: like the sound of many people breathing. A crowd is asleep behind this curtain. I am frozen in astonishment. Where am I? Am I still dreaming, having only imagined waking up? What kind of hotel is this Paradiso where people secretly sleep in large groups (to look at the hotel you would never suspect it) in a room apparently reserved for this purpose?

Without making a sound, I lift up a corner of the heavy tapestry. It is still totally dark but the breathing becomes more distinct, I can hear light quick breaths and heavy throat rattles ... Is there another curtain? At this point I go back into the hall, return to my room, and fall asleep dumbfounded.

The next day, when I go downstairs into the vibrant light, typical of this region with which I'm well acquainted—or so I thought—no one is at the front desk. During the day someone will explain to me that in fact the Paradiso provides rooms for the homeless people rounded up each night by the police.

Right now, nothing is certain. Did I dream the whole thing up?

AT THE HOSPITAL

Another collective sleep, but this particular one is troubled in such a way that it troubles me in turn, and at the same time clarifies something for me.

I am in the *Polyclinique* Hospital, where yesterday A. was urgently taken, and quickly operated on for a tumor the nature of which still remains unknown. He has regained consciousness, but the hospital staff is not sufficient to care for all of the critical patients; friends and family of the sick take shifts at night on cots and folding chairs next to their beds. We are in the emergency ward. Ninety people—ninety men—were operated on today, either for terrible illnesses or because of serious accidents. They sleep, or do not. On my cot, almost at floor level, I can't see much—the beds are very high, but I listen; and I hear something that both does and does not astonish me, but which, in this enormous room, and articulated by such a large number of voices, takes on a strange aspect, part concert, part proclamation. All these men in their agitated sleep, groan, cry, murmur, breathing the same word: *mama*. They are of all ages—a little earlier I saw some very old men—and probably come from every social background. They suffer, they call for *mama*. It resembles a disarming demonstration, almost comic in its obviousness.

Ancient chorus: the ninety sleepers.

SACRED SLEEP

The grandmother quietly reads before her daughter and her grandson, Jean-Paul Sartre:

"My mother stopped talking and asked me to be quiet, I thought of mass, of death, and of sleep. I filled myself with a sacred silence."

Mass, death, sleep: all things that impose silence, and are difficult to understand. The sacred makes us immobile, puts a stop to undisciplined everyday life, and is always a bit disdainful of the child. Sleep is situated in the "death-mass" constellation: A sleeping person looks dead. Communication is blocked: Respect is obligatory, imposed.

Or perhaps the resemblance between terms suggests the reverse: after death, the father (his corpse) is thought to be asleep, far away. This results in a slightly chilling indistinguishableness. *Mass*: outward signs of respect, of awe. And a new term is added to the chain: *mass, death, sleep, reading*. A person who reads is like a person at mass, asleep, or dead, dead to active life, to improvisation, to liberty.

The mystery, therefore, of reading, which can, for the child who does not yet know how to read, extract the coloring of the day from the inaccessible (the book). Sartre again: His mother reads aloud. "Anne-Marie had me sit across from her, on my little chair; she bent over, lowered her eyelids, fell asleep. From this frozen face came a plaster voice. I went mad: Who was telling the story? Of what? And to whom? It was no longer my mother before me: not one smile, not one sign of complicity, I was exiled." Here sleep comes closer to dreams ("My mother *fell asleep* and dreamt") than to death or paralyzing immobility. The speaker's "exile" points to what

Lacan called the "Three." Sleep, dreams, or reading, all reveal our solicitation of the other; or the change of an intimate, recognizable other into an other who observes.

The father is absent. Reading—a sleep-dream—becomes the father, that which pulls the child away from the all powerful mother and takes him somewhere else. The child will have to return to this place and conquer it on his own.

The sacred is also the secret, the secret of the mother, which awaits discovery. Little by little this paralyzing and dead constellation will become animated. The child will enter. One day, quickly, he will enter the forbidden sleep that has taken his mother away, and once there he will simultaneously find his mother and come to know this country—like the sea behind Albertine. But it will be a real departure. The mother, taking her charm (like Albertine), from the landscape, from the unknown country that surrounds her, is not here. She grows distant in this strange place, and the loving child follows suit—in spite of both of them, and with the consent of both.

As in daily life, falling asleep (here, by reading) is a prelude to departure. It begins with physical gestures and rites ("sat me down, bent over, lowered her eyelids"), followed by a dreamlike metamorphosis (frozen face, voice of plaster, surrealist images; Buñuel or Cocteau). Dreams infinitely distance us; they bring us close to death and the unknown.

"I went mad": absence, and inquiry. Already the philosopher at work: "Who is telling the story"? "where from"?—doubled by the vertiginous love of the child: "Where has my mother gone"? and to whom is she speaking? (certainly not me). The exile begins. It will be a question of finding a way out. "Books are for both of us!"

THE BLANK VOICE

When little Marcel's mother, having yielded, reads *François le Champi* to him to put him to sleep, the scene is quite different. Here the blank reading voice is not made of "plaster." It is life, and breath: "In a uniform rhythm, she breathed into this prose a kind of ongoing emotional life."

The child, the listener, already has an intense and dreamy relationship to books: He already knows how to enter the mysterious universe of literature. And what he discovers in his mother's bedtime reading, apart from the sweet sound of her voice, which embodies the nearby presences, before the frightening desert of approaching night (sleep, like solitude, is terror itself)—in addition to that something "indefinable" and "delicious" that books possess and make known to him—is proof of a profound relationship between her voice and his beloved books: "It furnished (the mother's voice) ... all of the ample sweetness which they demanded to these sentences which stayed completely within the register of her sensibility ... . She found, by tackling them in the right tone, a warm intonation that preexisted and dictated them, and which the words themselves had failed to indicate."

Here we are not in the stupor, nor the mortifying frost, we are in the vivacity of musical interpretation. The world has been provisionally unified. The "sad nocturnal hours" transfigured. An unrecoverable happiness which will be subsequently made into the model of happiness itself, and in the memory of which he will attempt, from thence forward, to produce "spiritual equivalents."

REAL MEANING

At the heart of the absence and death that we experience when asleep, or while watching someone else sleep, dreams provide us with whole, and therefore comforting, images: The individual, being itself, despite appearances, is perpetuated during sleep by producing these shapes ... which can be anguishing, even menacing, but do not undermine the dreamer's identity, which is the premise behind them all, their inventor and puppeteer, the omnipresence, the live center.

Except in those dreams with images of sleep. Then, suddenly, they crumble like Etruscan friezes exposed to air and view. Sleep, author of these images, destroys them. Sleep, like a dark corridor between two lights, is threatened by them and threatens them in turn.

Is a sleep dream the same as a death dream? Is this how dreams bring sleep's real meaning to light? Even if dreams need sleep to exist?

"The 'I' never thinks of itself as an effect."

And here's the big news—to consider it as such, the moment it sleeps and dreams.

MISE EN SCÈNE

Sleep is childhood's great mise en scène. It works, collates, and annexes images and episodes.

I had a childhood desire that came from books to have a grandmother like those I had read about who recount stories to help you fall asleep. Mine never told stories. Tender and long-suffering, she never stopped asking and waiting for some proof of our love, which we gave but rarely, and in any case never enough. We were gripped by a vague unformulated fear of finding ourselves somehow swallowed into the disquieting abyss hidden in her excess of affection. She knitted white socks for us out of a sort of thick lace, and wanted us to try them on. We had to stop in the middle of a race or a game, cautiously glide our feet into the fragile sheath while the cold needles pressed against our skin, wait, take them off, always with great care. Instead of giving ourselves over to these fittings, we chased each other faster and faster around the table where she sat waiting for us. "My God, these children will kill themselves," she groaned, and her worry excited us even more. Our tenderness for her was unspoken, and at any rate was not fully felt until after she had passed away.

One afternoon when I was ill—I was almost always ill during this period—the others had gone out, but my father was working in his study; when he came to check on me, I asked him to read me a story from the book I had gotten for Christmas, a few days earlier. He kindly set about reading the story.

He was not a grandmother, and the story wasn't being recounted, only read; and it was not nighttime, the true time of solemnity, but just plain afternoon. While the voice of my father read, I forced the various parts of the situation to conform to my desired image of it. I did not know how to describe the sound of this reading voice, this calm and cultivated voice which pronounced French with justice and transparency—measured and slightly separated from the sentences it read, reserved and ironic. A tongue from time to time visited by brief golden flashes of Burgundian pronunciation—with the irregular hint of a rolled r.

In fact, I do not remember one thing about the content of this unique reading session—only the scene and my febrile effort to turn it into the grandmotherly image and voice from books that I longed for. This effort erased both what I was listening to, and all memory of it.

The reading did not last long. The others returned from their walk, reddened with cold, tea was made, my father, relieved, disappeared once more into his study, my mother took up, with her habitual quickness—there was never a question of interrupting her, for example, by asking for a story—the reins of the large house. And I, my alibi of the sick-bed renewed, returned to reading, alone, in a soft voice—in the protective solitude, managing around me a large space of smooth and unified time, delivered, by my illness, from fragmentation, walks, school: a time during daylight as smooth and capacious as that of night ...

DAWN OVER THE SEA

Awakened very early in the morning, I struggle in half-consciousness to block out the voices of the fishermen on the dock below. What should I do? Cover my ears with the quilt and return as fast as I can to the beneficent land of sleep? Or rather, go out on the balcony, listen to the voices, and watch this extraordinary countryside waking up? The reflection of the dock lamps still illuminates the calm and somber water; in the distance, below and to the left, a pink glimmer slowly brightens a black line of clouds bordering the sea, while the rest have turned almost white. One by one the barks pull away from the bank, heading toward the hesitant sun. It is as if a cortège of boats has been charged to bring the loiterer into port ... the large ones depart with loud buzzing motors alternating with voices—barked orders, jokes, exchanges that, while difficult to make out, are regulated and rhythmic. A great and singular rhythm seems to carry the boats over the glimmering water, distributing their trajectories, their successive movement and dispersion over the expanse.

Why do I feel that sleep, so nearby, still warm in the bed behind me, has suddenly become immobilized, relegated to the darkness, to a casket, to dull death? What seemed to me, not an instant ago, a tender and nourishing refuge, from which I was torn by annoying voices, has transformed into the thing that tried to prevent me from witnessing this sight, this miracle—the birth of a star.

It appears suddenly, perfectly round, bright and crimson—then all becomes roseate while, very rapidly now, it climbs ... then suddenly, a new metamorphosis, no longer merely resplendent, it lights up the world. In the still somber room the window latch is a pink-gold and the wall is tinged orange. Below, on the dock, two cats watch the last boats leave, the small ones, the ones that will arrive too late ... the gull cries enter the room, they cry high above while criss-crossing, their movements partake in the rhythmic totality.

Sleep returns. Like an eraser, like a foggy emptiness that sucks up all color, like a meal awaiting you on the table ... soft bed, daytime sounds, someone is humming, the words gently drift up to the room, separated, suspended: *"Nel – sol – caliente."*

HARNESSING SLEEP

In some texts, the slippage from *soleil* (sun) to *sommeil* (sleep)—and, the even bolder case of *sommeil* to *soleil*—happens in a scene about falling asleep. Proust describes Apollo's mythological chariot. Here the brother of Hypnos is not Thanatos, but rather the god of light: "The horses of sleep, like those of the sun, move with such a measured step through an atmosphere so free of resistance that it would take the hurling of a small cosmic pebble ... to disrupt ..."

Proust perceives the language as a poet would, directly, and his writing foregrounds the proximity of sleep and sun as evoked by the French words. Sleep, like Apollo, drives a chariot pulled by horses. And the horses of the sun who had left their hoof-prints in the clearing near Illiers where the grass, burned in rings, and the presence of a seedling with immense yellow discs, called, justly, *suns*, makes the little Jean Santeuil believe that a god has just passed by: "He thought also of this spectacle as some kind of entrance into the Kingdom of the Sun where all was consecrated to the sun, where only sun flowers grew, and where the sun loved to go, with its mysterious horses."

In the *Search*, in a bold slippage, Apollo's chariot becomes that of Hypnos, and the narrator its driver: "Thinking we have taken just a short nap, we've slept away the entire day. In the chariot of sleep we descend to such depths that even the mind is obliged to turn back, and memory cannot follow us."

Letting its guard down, the mind makes irrational connections between one thing and another—founded on neither sense nor reasoning. Homonymy generally belongs to this decelerated angle of thought. Synonymy, it stands to reason, is sheltered by the grand justification of analogy—which perhaps, if carefully examined, also makes allowance for some sleepiness and slippage.

Some tropes are proud, more or less, more or less noble and certain. Metaphor expands the horizon, brightening it as it rises, and establishes well-founded connections, which we accept without hesitation or objection, with the instinctive recognition that we grant a person who guides us through an unfamiliar city. Metonymy, by contrast, pressures tenuous relationships based on actual proximities, which are more often than not simply neighbors by chance, sometimes born by a usurping substitution—to "have a glass." What defines metonymy as distinct from other tropes is its claim to "bridge the gap." It is the pillow of our sleep, which takes us "there where all knowledge becomes slightly disfigured."

HEADLESS AND SHY

From the first signs of sleep the neck muscles, which hold the head upright on the body, cease functioning. A gentle guillotine, sleep turns us all into would-be decapitants—though without the pride of André Masson's mythic drawing on the cover of Bataille's magazine *Acéphale*. There the headless athletic body of a calm rebel warrior pulses with strength—his legs and arms symmetrically outspread, like Leonardo's Vitruvian man, a measure of the universe, his acephalic state seems to increase his power, reason extends throughout his body—the skull moved down, coiled exactly where the genitals should be. A new measure, violent, and in its way tranquil.

Sleeping, falling asleep, we are nothing but shy headless bodies, a spectacle of renunciation and submission. You listen to the talk, you progress little by little through the light and knowledge, meanwhile I am felled under your gaze—an animal mimicking submission before a more dominant animal—I display my submission to the powers of night, and death, which win out.

Through sleep, every day we relive the defeat of our thought, the defeat of the supremacy of our experience. Every day the moment I fall asleep eludes me: fall, lapse, I can never say, "I'm falling asleep." The verb "*s'endormir*" (to fall asleep) does not conjugate in the first person of the indicative present.

Sleep soon inserts us into a kind of shattered thought. We are the playthings of illusions. Illusions that are not attached to an object or another angle of perception, but to the "ego." This is not about the "sleep of reason" which breeds monsters. It's "a rather peculiar turn of reflection." Reason is not offended. It's just forgotten. Every day we forget poor reason. We become haunted by beliefs. But in sleep-dreams the simultaneity of diverse beliefs prevents the believer's usual confusion. A game emerges. Sleep as critic?

THE SLEEP-DREAM BLOC

When, in the sleep-dream bloc, sleep gives dreams the advantage—marvels, expansiveness, figures, mysteries—the sleeper loses track of who masters and projects them. As in the first vision of the *Vita Nuova* when Love cradles in its arms the naked beloved wrapped in a red sheet: "How happy Love seemed, holding my heart in its hand / with my lady, wrapped in a sheet / sleeping in its arms."

Sleep is the master of slippage. It moves the gaze to its margins (waking-dream) and disappears behind them. But dreams take their authority from sleep, as well as their prestige and their "incontestable" air. Dreams, but perhaps also all stories. The power of story has its origin in dreams, and dreams in sleep.

"Without sleep dreams would be nothing but slightly incoherent reveries, a bit fantastic. They would remain fluid and docile."

SLEEP WITH A CAT

Pamino the cat installs himself on the pillow for the night, slightly above my head, to the left. Sitting nobly, purring, two paws placed on the top of my arm. It feels a bit like passing the night at the feet of the lion of Belfort. Watched over and protected by an animal god, who also, it's true, keeps me awake, with his little contentment motor.

But then I remember that purring can signify either satisfaction or anxious emotion, intense worry, and fear. When the cat Ptung was bringing her litter into the world, her purring continued, almost obsessively, until the very end, a propitiating and protective rhythm; the anxiety and the suffering made manifest nevertheless by her need for a constantly attentive and uninterrupted human presence.

Pamino, despite his growing beauty—more and more the lion, more and more the tiger—and his intelligence, ever more wise, tender and quick (one dreams of a similar transformation in humans), is a very old cat; and what I interpret as a sign of pleasure and of satisfaction might actually be an expression of pain and worry. "Pamino, do your teeth hurt?" I am awake; dawn is filtering through the blinds. Someone, very nearby, keeps watch—or sleeps?—immobile, the head straight, small and somber, his two paws resting firmly on my arm.

SLEEP WITH A BABY

For several days now, he moves—slowly passing, almost insensibly, from one wall to the other, the movements of a smothered swim, as if he prefers to remain undetected, anonymous—a night dancer's gestures, or an expert hotel thief. A discreet acrobat lives inside of me, he would like to be forgotten, to melt into the furniture.

Or, on the spur of the moment, a skillfully discharged kick, an ill-tempered kick, mischievous, a sort of wink—the only kind of wink he is permitted, ultimately. "You've forgotten about me … but I'm here, increasingly. I'm getting ready. I'm coming."

I've known about him for some time now, ever since he made his presence known, very clearly, using a new kind of sleep as his introduction. There are certainly as many kinds of sleep as there are plants in a garden; heavy sleep, light, imperceptible sleep, interrupted, inaccessible, summer sleep, exhausted by the sun, or shadowy and wind-beaten winter sleep, intense, humming like a fire, fatigued sleep, energetic sleep … This one was new to me. It arrived in one stroke, but was very gentle, as gentle as a wing, and it quickly lifted me very far away, into a calm and porous substance, completely surrounded by air. This is how the invisible child brought me into his sleep, which I drank like milk.

SLEEP, FATIGUE, THOUGHT

In mystical writings, but also for example in Dante ("I was full of sleep at this point"), the word "sleep" is synonymous with an empty torpor, with an absence and emptiness of mind, since mind is, precisely, "wakefulness." Catherine of Siena: "Get up, get up, gentle Father, and sleep no longer. Because I hear such news that I no longer desire a bed or rest."

Modernity, distanced from the idyll between the romantic soul and dreams, and having left the surrealist obsession with the "royal road to the unconscious" behind, draws in a bit closer, and a bit more directly, to the reign of Hypnos.

And yet, in Georges Bataille's work the word "sleep" is probably, out of all words, the clearest marker of refusal, of categorical exclusion—so rare beneath a pen which endlessly doubles back on itself, corrects, opens never-before-thought-of relationships, points to unexpected analogy, dislocates the known term—all too known—by viewing it from another angle, where it convenes with other words, words which are not part of its habitual entourage; and creates a different associative chain—a brand new landscape.

There is another word in his writings—related to the word "sleep"—which is always the index of a vital resistance, a kind of knot which, though it looks like resignation or abandonment, in fact signals a kind of doubling-back of thought, an entanglement that fosters unexpected depth, necessary and unique: the word "fatigue."

The "fatigued" character, the one who is felled very suddenly by exhaustion (*Blue of Noon*), is the character that matters. Others, those unfamiliar with this crash, this intermission, continue to cart out light, weightless, and recycled reasoning.

The slowing down, the momentous emptiness of mind, confusion even, forms a kind of nest where awakening can emerge. The journey through torpor and stupidity is necessary—better still: It is fertile. A thought that has not known interruptions, short circuits, fleeting but significant black-outs, cannot know itself, and will be tarnished by this naiveté, this goodwill, responsible for reducing many a philosophical enterprise to academicism and, in the end, uselessness.

The strange mechanism of synonymy that Bataille introduces into his language is here made manifest. Thus thinking that is too light, that never falls, becomes for him synonymous with what he terms, in connection to Sartre, "slow thinking."

And the idea of "speed," which he reclaims for his own thought, is what we would call "animal"—the movements of sleep and dreams included—it is uncontrolled. Abrupt sleep, like an angel falling with its sword, figure of the necessary nose-dive.

THE SEVEN SLEEPERS

Seven Christian youths of Ephesus, to escape having to worship pagan idols under the Emperor Decius, hide out in a cave. After finding that they have been sealed up alive with their dog Carenc, they fall asleep.

They sleep for three hundred and nine years, while the dog, legs stretched out, keeps watch. At the end of three hundred and nine years, they wake up for several hours and serve as proof of the resurrection. Having thus been able to set an example of the triumph of divine justice, they quickly die. "The mysterious sleep is a rocking like that of a boat on the ocean—a boat of salvation, abandoning oneself to God—in an instant faith" (Massignon).

Arthur Rimbaud might be called the "eighth sleeper" (Salah Stétié). In him reigned this ancient idea of sleep (as opposed to the mystic's notion of spiritual inertia) as a "retreat," a plentitude gained by the "spiritual curvature of time." There is an awareness at the core of sleep: It is a matter, finally, of "putting ourselves to sleep so that the other behind the I can emerge."

All types of sleep and awakening belong to him, and he defines them: "enlightened rest," sleep "in a nest of flames," "I realized that my soul slept," "yet was sleepless." "At the same time he knows and does not, he knows he is asleep ... he knows that he is not in the world. His sleep is ... a falling asleep, a sleep in the flower of waking, an awakened sleep."

Paradisal sleep: The idea of paradise, as connected to sleep, shows up in the very first writings of Arthur the schoolboy. "The sun was still hot / ... a cool wind agitated / the leaves of the tree with a rustle / scattering ... the wind, I fell asleep, but not / before drinking water from the stream." Perfect countryside, where all is responsive, where sleep is enthroned; just like in the forest "thick and alive" at the summit of Purgatory, where the visit is made possible by taking a drink (of water from Lethe).

This is also Rimbaud's intuition about the nature of his own sleep: his sense not only of ambiguity or contradiction, but also of *reversal*. Sleep is "awakened by sleep," in a movement of lightening speed, which seizes the essence of sleep, and approaches the heart of thought.

TIME

Afternoon, after a storm, on the tip of a deserted cape: white stones in a semi-circle at the base of a little lighthouse, its vertical lines against a sky of very intense blue. The vast plane of the sea a perfectly smooth, symmetrical blue. In the distance, on the horizon, to the left, two large white boats draw near little by little, the one very quickly, the other almost imperceptibly, but not so as their movements affect in any way the unchanging, so to speak, impression of the scene.

So little in fact that I experience the change of light suddenly produced by another, smaller, boat, in the background, next to a silvery zone stretching out toward the right, the silver color not cloud-based—the sky remains as essentially pure as before—but a result of the changing afternoon light, like a shock to the heart, like a gong—like a failure of the entire visible plain ...

What can escape this change, this decline wrought by time? Sleep can, in a way. Perhaps it has a function that does not show up in the analysis of specialists. That of approaching the notion of timelessness, of eternity, if you wish, but in life, that of suggesting a substratum of time beneath the time that devours and changes all things, all landscape, rapidly and without recourse.

A noise in the olive grove awakens me, suddenly I'm pulled from my cocoon of safety and brought into the jerky, plodding, exhaustion of time filled with threats and events (thieves, the storm, summer's end) ... And yet still I dimly sense, surrounded by the busy darkness, that the time-space the noise drew me out of wasn't merely an escape from these real things (or imaginary, but imaginary in the time of consciousness). Rather, just the opposite, it was a place more profound, more real, and more capable of reading the tormenting aspects of being awake than the waking state itself, thanks to the smooth, inaccessible, and detached shore of sleep.

Nighttime, in Greece, sleeping on the roof of the Patmos house. Every so often I awake and look up to see the stars very near my eyes, just above my head, but at each awakening I see a different vista, a new configuration: I realize that while I've slept the sky has entirely shifted. First I think: Sleep has denied me the totality, the continuity of marvelous movement made by this celestial canopy. Secondly: But without sleep I would never have been able to capture such a vast and quasi-imperceptible displacement. It is sleep, with its astonishing gaps, that has given it to me.

Thirdly: Isn't sleep itself in some strange harmony with this overall movement? Once each cycle making me open my eyes in order to see the great circle where I am sleeping, waking up, and falling asleep once more, this time right before early morning, before the dew, the air still pale before the sun and the fresh figs on the very small trees around the house—at the same time sensing, for now, the light of the stars and the warmth of the sleeping bag, to which I return and continue to turn with it and with the universe, so long as they are connected.

SLEEP SHINES

The very last light of sleep, as it moves away:
    Dante: "As sleep ruptures when suddenly, / a ray of light strikes your closed eyes / and then, severed, shines brightly before dying out."

ALL MUST DISAPPEAR

Having barely emerged from the darkness, I see something being drawn like an image—less an image, more an idea, a pain, the outline of a judgment—something connected to the previous day, which I thought sleep had put behind me. It's as if the live center of this day had, in its final hours, resisted the enterprise of being forgotten and transformed by the great digestive chemistry of dreams. Right now I feel as if its center is lodged somewhere in my benumbed body—the location of this pure emergence is vague, and at times painful. Is this what woke me up?

I sense this day's violence now deposited in my muscles, a trace of its aggression and a trace of my own excess. My excess is like a too-loud injurious voice. My too-loud voice of yesterday damages the start of this new day. I must, half-asleep, quickly quiet it. With an everyday gesture I only vaguely discern, as if deftly wielding a mysterious eraser, I remove it without moving or opening my eyes; a decision, a kind of resolution made on the spot without my full consent.

No more excess of presence, no more cumbersome parts of me floating up to the surface. Softness, the lightness of days, taking their cue from this moment when, though barely awake, I no longer cling to night, or to my fading dream, or to sleep's silence. I hear a voice telling me: Days have their own music, including this day that is just beginning.

When I wake up a bit more this all disappears, is erased. In one go, I wake up from both sleep and dreams—from the mass of dreams still pressing on my eyelids. All must disappear. The new day demands every bit of space, clean, and entire. At breakfast, it struggles already with a cumbersome bit of memory, like a stale chewy croissant insistently returning to the mouth.

THE SLEEP OF ZARATHUSTRA

Sleep has sovereignty—it plays with time, causing more hours to drift over the sleeper's face than he intended when he lay down. It astonishes and disconcerts him and then opens his eyes to the silence of the surrounding nature. Then, it gives him a gift, which makes him leap up. In this leap, sleep gives birth to awakening—it invents it, it is it. And the awakening is the birth of an idea:

"Zarathustra slept a long time; not only did the dawn's light pass over his face, but that of the morning as well. Finally he opened his eyes: With astonishment Zarathustra looked out at the forest and into the silence, with astonishment he looked into himself. Then he leapt up, like a sailor suddenly discovering land, and he let out a cry of joy: because he saw a new truth."

Enlightenment born of night, a sailor who sees land, gaiety: "Sleep got me to thinking." Nourishing, and more than nourishing: creative. It is important to remember this Zarathustra, the leaping sailor who is capable of confiding in the sun, and who extracts his new ideas, those he prefers, directly from sleep (and who is the opposite of the right-thinking, mannered, and occultist character he is usually thought to be).

Completely contrary to the bloated image of the superman this new idea is as follows: "I need companions, living companions" ... "Companions, that is what the creator seeks ... creators like himself... "

Thus sleep incites something beyond dreams, beyond shining and desirable images. It sneaks up, suddenly bringing into daylight the most powerful structures of thought, that lift it up, and will soon carry it away...

THE SLEEP OF ODYSSEUS

When sailing for Ithaca, at last, "a delicious sleep, without fretfulness and full of sweetness, very like death, fell over the eyelids of Odysseus."

Sweet and delicious, and "very like death." When, soon after arriving on shore, he tells the story of his adventures to the goddess (who is disguised as a young shepherd) this sleep will be the only part with any truth to it. With the exception of this one moment, "A sweet sleep overtook me, so worn out was I with exhaustion," he falsifies and reverses the story of his adventures. Pressure point that authors the spirit of the narrative: "In and among the network of events he bears on his shoulders there is one, like a crimson thread, to recount truthfully; everything else can be changed, elaborated, reversed, being truthful about his sweet sleep and his arrival is enough."

On numerous Greek vases and on the chest of Kypselos at Olympia, Hypnos and Thanatos are represented as twin brothers in the arms of their mother, Night. One is black, the other white. Which is which? Death is white, sleep black.

Heraclitus: "Man lights a light in death, when his eyes / go out. While alive, he borders death when asleep. And borders sleep when awake.

Sleep is also the interval between one story and another, between Odysseus the storyteller and Odysseus the character. It's the break that contains a portion of death, like an antidote.

NOT OF THIS WORLD

Even those who do not like it will end by confronting and choosing it. Thus, Bataille:

"If I hadn't noticed right away, in the night, this feeling, I would have forgotten it. There's a way in which such states assume a loss of consciousness of the world's reality: I awoke from a sleep I was confident I would return to; in the inertia of the bed I was a life adrift which had a hold on nothing, and which nothing could hold onto."

Inexistence, insignificance. "Because they are not of this world we neglect such moments: their indifference, solitude, and silence do not get out attention, they reside there as if nonexistent (like a deserted mountain range)."

"We call such moments insignificant because they lack daytime's idea of sense, such as getting dressed, going out, putting things in order: Thus they are insignificant. Nor do they make sense the way dreams do, which are only daytime's sense rendered absurd: an absurdity so captivating it inhibits us from seeing this *nakedness*, this immense silent object, hiding, denying itself and, in hiding, revealing that everything else is a lie."

"Ennui" moves in; in other words, one must go through sleep to get to dreams, the rugged landscape where the law of production is the waking landscape turned absurd. Sleep is situated between these two domains: that of being awake, where we dress, go out, and "put things in order," and that of dreams, which is simply daytime displaced, mixed up, "disordered." Sleep undresses appearances; it is the void and "nakedness." Barely human, it does not speak to the soul. And yet, sleep shelters truth, letting us see that "everything else is a lie."

Here sleep is something else, something more than the pale provisionary double of death. It is the source—for those who can resist both the easy charms of dreams and the multiple distractions of being awake, for those who have, "by chance," set their gaze on the unquantifiable expanse of impoverished, "insignificant" time—of the very truth of human existence, which is the following: There is no secret, there is nothing but an empty void, without meaning, which nobody wants to know about, but sleep knows ...

This moment does not fit with Bataille's typical attitude: his impatience, his juvenile reaction against the "dormant," against drowsiness in general, as a figure of resignation, of mental inertia, and of spiritual death. Here sleep is seen as secret material, as central, as a kind of degree zero of the energy which menaces all things, which awaits its hour ... a figure of death if you wish, but it is life, life itself, infinitely small and intimate, as seen from the vantage point of its sister death.

THE SLEEPER AWAKENED

A rich young man, living with his mother, goes out nights to carouse with strangers. He avoids the first light of dawn, which provokes madness. Magically put to sleep, he awakens in the palace of the Caliph. At dawn's first light he goes mad and strikes his mother: "He got up abruptly and grabbed a club, going toward her with his hand raised up in fury: 'Accursed old woman,' he said to her, his extravagance striking fear in all others with gentle mothers, 'tell me, right away, who I am.'"

This story, from *A Thousand and One Nights*, told in this way, is the first model—emblem, medallion—for the series of "profaned mothers" in the *Search*. What it allows us to see, what it allows into the daylight, is the disturbing weight of night, so disturbing that going to sleep, which looks very easy, is actually the successful completion of a dangerous transition, steering us clear of enigmas and keeping us from coming unhinged, around the edges especially, at that moment of "first light" (which provokes deliria and the worst of regressions, the hateful regression against the mother). If sleep is not allowed to have its day, madness enters the scene. He who does not abandon himself to this moment of non-reason, of non-control, he who has forgotten to "go to bed early," falls prey to irrationality. Thus is revealed the dark underside of all filial love: hate, profanation, criminality, always waiting to surface...

Sleep protects. It keeps the human furies locked up, disabled, the way Aeolus kept the winds in his goatskin.

ENTRUSTING YOURSELF TO SLEEP

Entrusting yourself to sleep: a frightening act—J. D. telling me the other day that he almost never falls asleep without anxiously asking himself if he will wake up, if this inexplicable phenomenon will produce itself once more for him, or not.

Valéry: "How dare we go to sleep? What confidence in the reliability of my body, in the calm of night, in the order and constancy of the world!"

But it is also, as soon as we accept it, a humble and sensible act, which separates out the black truths, the insane truths, the terrible errant world of phantasms without faith or law ("Accursed old woman, tell me right away ... ").

There is, it's true, a secondary foolishness: the unconscious foolishness of the one who gives over to the "essential weakness" of sleep, that is to say to images, to dreams. Valéry again: "The alarming inexplicable powerlessness, the essential weakness and invincible spell which chains your closed eyes to these images."

From reason's standpoint (according to Valéry) sleep is powerless twice over, and twice over weak: because it delivers me over to the unconscious, because it has nothing more pressing to do than to enslave me to images and illusions.

NOBODY KNOWS

Yes, sleep enslaves me to an illusion.

But the illusion it's comprised of, and introduces, is possibly more clear-sighted than the distinct and level-headed opinions we employ in our vain attempts to oppose it. All life is a kind of sleep.

Pessoa: "Nobody knows what's up, nobody knows what is wanted, and nobody knows what is known. We are asleep in life, eternal children of destiny."

Going by that, following this train of thought, we arrive by degrees at the perfect synonymy of sleep-awareness and sleep awakening. "As if taking a walk, I sleep, but am awake. As if sleeping, I wake up, and don't know who I am. At bottom life is one long insomnia and everything we think and do is an abrupt, lucid awakening."

We are back to Rimbaud: There is an awareness at the core of sleep.

THE RIDICULOUS

The ridiculous always comes into relief with the approach of sleep, reducing to nothingness (to ridicule) our most grandiose efforts. George Bataille: "By writing I wanted to get to the bottom of things. And, having giving myself this task, I fell asleep."

But the ridiculous ends by allowing us to interrogate the essential, to reach "the limits of silence," the point where thought comes undone. Sleep ceases, therefore, to be the obstacle; it becomes, strangely, the end, or, perhaps, the sign—and even the model. "To speak of the poignant dissolution of thought at the limits of silence, slip gently into sleep."

CAN ONE LOVE AN INSOMNIAC?

In what way is sleep ultimately necessary to us? Simply for rest and the restoration of forces? For something more, undoubtedly: "After a night of sleeping poorly nobody loves us. Sleep brings with it something that makes us human" (Pessoa).

To be human is to lack, to desire dialogue, questions … Insomnia rips us from our fellows, from the community of tender sheep in the field. The other sheep—the humans—do not recognize us.

To be human is also, perhaps, the thing that allows us to imagine in a face, in a body, the potential for surrendering to enticements … love and sleep: Can one love an insomniac? What we love in a face, in a body, in the ways of inhabiting a body, is perhaps after all nothing more than its tendency—visible, revealed for nothing—from one moment to the next, to fall asleep, like a secret sensuality, like a promise of surrender. Thus F. F. reported, with bemused astonishment, a woman's confession to him that the thing about M., a friend they had in common, she found most remarkably seductive, most forcefully erotic, was his habit of wearing his watch band loosely floating around his wrist. What could this be a sign of, F. F. asked himself? Of a disposition so easily removed it is liable to let slide, in similar fashion, clothes off the body? Or simply of a mark of disinterest—a sensual nature—toward daily conventions, as if swept away by impatience, by a gust of wind, by absent-mindedness—an absent-mindedness that is, in its essence, a lover's, and shares with sleep the same nonchalant body beneath the other's gaze, knowingly exposing itself at the moment of its greatest unconsciousness: oblivious, offered? …

"His neck palpitated like the necks of the sleepers I once dreamed of … I moved my shadow over his cheeks and his mouth, in a kind of mysterious touch" (Julian Green).

A STRANGE PIECE OF FURNITURE

What a strange piece of furniture, this bed (called "matrimonial" in Italian) where two people, traditionally of the opposite sex, fall asleep together each night. Strange, because sleep—as rest and the restoration of forces, and therefore a complete interruption of social activities—should, it seems, permit isolation, a silent gathering up and a retreat, far away from other humans. The erotic act, or that of reproduction (however you wish to consider it) would better maintain its particularity this way, it would remain set apart, and not risk becoming flat, numbed by being mixed in with conjugal sleep, more and more conjugal, less and less loving.

On the other hand, the beds of Fragonard and Boucher, with their sheets light and rumpled like frothy roses, are true monuments to the sleep of love, as are those cavern-like places lined with mirrors for the god Hypnos in the mysterious abode of *No Tomorrow* by Vivant Denon; or Zuccari's frescoes in the palace of Caprarola, more tender and voluptuous than Ovid's *Metamorphoses*, where the god, surrounded on all of the furniture in his underground dwelling by images of dreams—his children—dangles his head and responds with great effort to the questioning visitor … . Half-real nymphs of Caprarola in the gesture of fleeing, but very soporifically. The eroticism of sleep comes from this doubt, this half-slowness, this sluggish unsuccessful slipping away … I am fleeing you but my thigh is intertwined with yours … what's happening? My eyelids fall. Trouble slips in. Is that your hand? Shells, waves, ebb and flow—all places we can neither access nor inhabit except in particular and precious circumstances, like this one. Distracted nymphs, silent fauns. In this shadowy grove we share an intimate glance.

Yet night begins in this piece of furniture, like an installation: knees tucked into knees, breath on neck, covers pulled up, air touching just the face, and the many arms which find their rightful place; adjustments, sighs, the entire ensemble turning itself over as one unit to the right or the left, night has begun. And on those days that, for one reason or another, are not preceded by this mélange (due to dreaded twin beds, for example) an emptiness forms, a coldness, a breach that will be prove difficult to mend.

There is, however, at least one loving matrimonial bed: the bed of Odysseus, which he built with his own hands out of a large olive tree growing up through the middle of his palace in Ithaca, like a great column, well planed and carved, finished with stones and ornamented with gold, silver, and ivory; and tightened with resplendent straps of crimson leather. "There is a great secret, he says, in this well-worked bed which I myself built, with the help of no one."

Perhaps his secret is at base only this: that for twenty years he has been away at sea. And so this marvelous bed, built for everyday life, is forever wedded to absence and nostalgia. At the same time, it's as if it has just been built—the reader only learns of the bed's existence at the end of the *Odyssey*, when Odysseus describes its construction in such a way as to make it seem like he has just finished the work. But as soon as he describes it, he fears that its foundation has been sawed off and moved elsewhere by the suitors who still occupy the palace.

The bed, in fact, is a secret: Nobody, except Odysseus, Penelope, and one servant, know of its existence. Bed of virginal love, bed of impossible sleep.

Barely having arrived, he leaves again. He goes inland, where passers-by won't recognize the oar he is carrying on his shoulder. He thus performs a mixture therefore of extremely familiar, quotidian acts—carrying an oar like a sailor walking through port, building a piece of furniture out of the wood of an olive tree like a peasant, sea and earth, worker and adventurer. The most quotidian (the matrimonial bed) is also the least present and the least accessible.

In the *Odyssey* Penelope weaves a great shroud by day and unweaves it by night. But she also sleeps, she sleeps a lot. When she cries, Athena puts her to sleep and sends her a dream. Penelope continues to sleep after Odysseus has arrived and is busy killing all the suitors.

And when the old nursemaid comes to announce the return of her husband, Penelope is still sleeping; she immediately and vehemently reproaches the old woman for waking her up: "It was the sweetest sleep that I have tasted since Odysseus went away." An expert taster of the many different types of sleep, where did she sleep all of this time? In the center of the palace in a bed which nobody knew about?

POETS

Amid the sleepers poets sound the buzzer on the alarm. They are, for humans who live drowsily in the shadows, the messengers of light: "O wake up the poet, and wake from sleep all those / who still slumber, give the laws" (Hölderlin).

Nighttime, which they illuminate, belongs to sleepers. It is the time when the gods grow distant.

But only darkness makes light possible; only sleep the possibility of waking. René Char: "When the mission is to wake up, you begin by bathing in the river." In the river Lethe, in the river Hypnos?

Appearance, and at the same time disappearance: leaves trembling in the winter sun, when the light cuts through the trees, almost horizontally. Andrea Zanzotto: it is always the *"animula vagula blandula"* that plays in the meadows, like Psyche plays with the lamp over the body of the sleeping Cupid. "Fear, he says, fear the true thoughts of those asleep."

From the porous sleep of morning arise the first words of the poem (*"o miei dolci animali"*), as if having come through the air, from another unknown poem, a kind of pebble to be polished with the tongue. But, smoother than all others, it keeps its secret.

Perhaps sleep without dreams is the true poetic condition. Sleep more distant than dreams.

PLAY

A story from adolescence of waking up on a Sunday morning at Maisons-Laffitte:

the day when they awoke on the sagging couches beneath the windows, the beating of a violent yet brief rain—outside the garden is dry and of the most intense green they've ever seen, sleep deprivation stopping and firmly holding them against the back of what they see: an unsought-for harmony found, from that moment on the day's course unfolded with efficacious ordered diffusion until finally it reached that floating forgetfulness in which this moment could recover its rightful weight of absence (its equivalent): waking up under the windows and going out into the garden sleep itself realized by the position of this isolated trembling revelatory moment above all about what if not about something—what—about waking up very early the cloud burst the going out into the empty garden the demolishing diverting active day before us—and forgetfulness the only thing strong and true enough to reestablish the exact weight of this moment so that it will not continue to be lost

Schelling: "If a light came up at night, if a nocturnal day and a diurnal day could embrace us all, it would be the supreme end of every desire."

From which: marvel of the night lit up by the moon—quivering presentiment of another life—at last *double*.

DOUBTS

The learned interrogate the enigma of sleep, but it persists, and at times the learned become discouraged, and filled with doubt. Thus Allan Rechstaffen:

"Perhaps sleep has no function. Perhaps we should resolve ourselves to accepting that our inability to isolate a specific function for sleep is proof that this function does not exist. But it is difficult to believe that we pass a third, or nearly, of our lives in a state that serves no function."

It is difficult for the learned to doubt science. He continues:

"It is difficult to believe that the merciless pressure that pushes us toward sleep whenever we have been deprived of it is not the work of a indispensable and sensitive system, ready to react with strength and speed whenever we are in need."

Little by little the learned begins to doubt nature:

"If sleep doesn't serve an absolutely vital function, it constitutes the greatest error ever committed by the evolutionary process. Because sleep prevents the hunt and therefore the consumption of food, it also makes us vulnerable to attacks from our enemies. Sleep fetters every voluntary motor act of the adaptation mechanism ... "

At this point he makes a hypothesis: Perhaps sleep is a fossil, and natural selection a failure:

"Is it not therefore but a residue which has outlived its functional utility ... a monstrous useless vestige, poorly adapted, over the long evolution of mammals, while natural selection has been capable, during the same period, of making all sorts of delicate and precise harmonious adjustments for the better, such as the form of the fingers and toes?"

Nature nods … and so does the learned one.

THE OTHER APARTMENT

"It has its servants, and its visitors. Right now they're on their way over to pick us up for a night out. We are almost ready when we are suddenly transported into the real apartment—the daytime one. The room is empty. We can no longer pretend that visitors are coming over. The race that lives in the "other" apartment, like the first humans, is androgynous. A man can without a moment's notice suddenly turn into a woman. Things there have an aptitude for becoming human, both as friend and foe."

Some dreams, those which, upon waking, make us feel temporarily joyful and then singularly deceived, lead us to believe that we own, beyond our familiar walls, one to several supplementary rooms, rooms we previously didn't know about or unduly neglected. They seem familiar upon entering, and we feel admiration for the natural ingeniousness of their arrangement. Our pleasure in them is similar to the one we took in large house mirrors when we were children, imagining that there was an exact replica of the house we were in on the other side of the mirror, where perhaps, at that very moment, our childhood double was walking the very same walk and asking the very same questions.

Couldn't the rooms we discover in dreams also be an image—formed by dreams themselves—of this "other apartment," which we enter each night when asleep, forsaking our own?

THE EAST

In Indian thought, sleep is sometimes judged negatively:

"Son of Bharata! Know that the inclination to separate yourself flows from ignorance. It tricks the living and binds them with negligence, laziness, and sleep."

Thus sleep is placed on the same level as religious cults that want to keep man imprisoned in the chains of existence, and whose gods are the deceptive energies:

"Whoever loves a god other than the Immensity and thinks: 'He is one, I am other,' is ignorant. He is like a head of cattle to the gods. Each living being is useful to the gods as cattle are useful to men. If even one cow is removed, it's disagreeable. What would we say if many were removed? That's why man's knowledge is disagreeable to the gods."

But there is another reading of sleep—more precisely of "deep sleep"—when considered in connection with two other states: awareness and dreaming.

Deep sleep, the inactive state of Consciousness, is the perception of happiness.

Dreamless sleep is connected to Shiva, the God of sleep, who resides in the middle of the forehead, the center of abstraction, as well as in the genitals, the center of pleasure.

A complete silencing of thought leads us to the highest degree of consciousness, the perfect happiness of pure existence. From the standpoint of human achievement, Shiva represents the final dissolution of the individual.

Thus the hierarchy of the three qualities varies depending on how you look at them. From the standpoint of human action, sleep is the inferior aspect, wakefulness the superior. Where only action seems to get results, sleep looks like death, evil, inaction. While from the standpoint of spiritual realization, where action is the primary obstacle, wakefulness is the inferior aspect, sleep the superior, for it liberates through non-action.

SNOW

"It was late at night when K. arrived. The village was covered in a thick snow."

The entire story of *The Castle* is a dream. From the opening lines forward each sentence is pulled inside another logic, the logic of dreams. The reader has neither the time nor the right to a moment's rest, nor can they awaken —"it was only a dream"— from this reasoning, these visions, these controlled presences to the familiarity of their own bed and thoughts.

Instead of breaking the continuity of the sleep-dream fabric—as dreams and their narrators typically do—the dream in this case has a different quality: It retains the substance of sleep.

And snow is the sign of this substance. It weighs on K. and the village, but nowhere else. "It also seemed less deep on the mountains than in the village where K. had had so much trouble walking down the main road the day before. The snow was piled up to the windows of the cabins and weighed heavily on the low-slung roofs, while up there, on the mountain, all had a disengaged air."

"She tells her love while half-asleep / In the dark hours / With half-words, whispered low. / As Earth stirs in her winter sleep / And puts out grass and flowers / Despite the snow / Despite the falling snow" (Robert Graves).

In other places—further south (in ancient Rome)—sleep is not snow but water. It is called *"liquidus somnus"*: "Sleep fled the hollow horn … like in paintings, when liquid sleep is poured from a horn over the sleepers" (Lactance). And in his *Force de Dormir* Pierre Pachet notes that throughout Kafka's writing, not just in *The Castle*, snow and sleep are often linked, but usually through a "dream vision." Breezy, easeful thinking, the happiness that comes from well being. To Max Brod upon seeing some skiers:

"There are some skiers across the way practicing going down the slope ... for them there is neither incline, nor ditch, nor slope, they glide over the landscape like a pen over paper ... : this is how a well-balanced man slips into sleep."

WHEN THE SENSE IS SLEEP

Maybe what literature must accomplish before falling silent, its true desire, is sleep, the exact moment of falling asleep.

"In *Ulysses*, to illustrate the mumblings of a woman falling asleep, I wanted to finish with the weakest word I could find. I settled on the word 'yes,' which is barely pronounced, which signifies acquiescence, abandon, truce, the end of all resistance. In the *Work in Progress*, I looked for better, if I could find it. This time, I found the most slippery word, the least accentuated, the most feeble in the English language, a word that isn't even a word, that barely makes a sound between the teeth, a breath, a nothing, the article '*the*.'"

In *Ulysses*, it is a woman who falls asleep *(yes)*. In *Finnegans Wake*, it is the entire language, which, having run the gamut, enters the sea with the river Liffey, a feminine dissolution into the original feminine element. But here the feminine doesn't correspond to fullness, to presence, to the earth and the all-enveloping. The allusion and goal is the moment of dissolution, the Nothing—the perfection of Nothing.

And the entire journey through the various languages, and all of the work, as well as the endless play on writing and sound was undertaken solely to discover the borders of words, where they end and turn into music, where language finally destroys itself and is transformed.

Out of the darkness, Beckett's voice:
  "*When the sense is sleep, the words go to sleep.*"

VIOLENCE

One day—one night—with the same yet different lover, since love is always new—I wake up and he's already inside me, going through the motions and struggle of love-making, and says, quietly, his mouth against my forehead, these bizarre words: "what butchery!" with a kind of incomprehensible desolation in his voice. I take in these words, and realize that he senses this loving assault on my sleeping body as a kind of rape, for which he apologizes to me in a gentle voice. But the apology pushes me away and my pleasure is diminished, erased; I liked my sleep blindness, the violent gestures, strangely slowed, strangely accentuated—as if underwater—as if we had reached an innocent but deep animal core. Familiarity is abolished, pleasure flees, he had been there, so close to the unconscious, and to heavy sleep.

ABSENCE

I tell myself this is how I could resolve—should resolve, perhaps—the irritating problem of whether or not to make love during an intense and fleeting relationship, which from the first has avoided and circumvented the act. A shared decision, which is perhaps neither shared, nor a decision: our avoidance settling variously on me and then him, in one sex and then the other, as is typical. We act as if our reasons are the same, because the first demand of all love (with or without the act) is perfect symmetry. Finally what's the difference between action and avoidance: "I ... you"— "yes, me too." A lie—it never comes out this way, not exactly.

Sometimes it can be very beautiful to *not* go all the way. One is therefore, each time, at the start, anticipating, with a tension that doesn't let up. But also racked with doubt: The avoidance becomes a sign of tepidness, prudence, or fear; and what if, when put to the test, our connection becomes overwhelming, and risks cutting our life threads, very slowly and arduously woven and unwoven. Or the opposite happens, we run aground, and this sort of casting out nines, or initiatory act—the longer delayed the more desired—proves insignificant or, who knows, embarrassing, deceptive, missed?

I propose, therefore, the following: Make love while asleep or, if it's possible, have already done it while asleep—or maybe just have dreamt it—but at the same time.

We're right back at the impossible, because we dream only for ourselves.

Perhaps, finally, just sleeping together is enough ...

One autumn morning in the train, heads together—two slightly hard boxes sliding against each other, not for long, just right before we arrive and must face the pain of separation. But this silly moment in the packed train—a silly but powerful moment—will serve as sustenance for the absence ahead. Sleeping together—absence doubled, and its opposite.

LOVE

Nighttime, my eyes suddenly open, he's beside me, perfectly still, leaning on his elbow, watching me—what pure happiness, to feel yourself the object of a gaze, an eyeless envelope, like a stone in the sea.

The happiness of being a watched stone—at once both stone and wave. I feel no embarrassment, nor like I'm being reduced to an object.

Voluptuous eroticism—a daytime gift—is quite distinct from this pleasure, though it too is made up, in some part, of this: to feel like an object beneath a gaze.

In this sense, the time we sleep belongs to love, to its nourishing energy. In watching me sleep, you protect me; you give me life. You are watching my life at its smallest: You see me as a child—a child yourself, but without that fragile equality, always at risk, and combativeness of children at play.

The space we are in is vast and without worry.

No adults in view.

Limbs intertwined, we go to sleep …

BY JACQUELINE RISSET

BOOKS
Jeu
L'Anagramme du désir : essai sur la Délie de Maurice Scève
La Traduction commence
Dans la barque dorata
Dante écrivain ou l'Intelletto d'amore
Sept passages de la vie d'une femme
L'Amour de loin
Marcelin Pleynet (Poètes d'aujourd'hui)
L'Annonce faite à Federico
Petits éléments de physique amoureuse
Dante: une vie
Puissances du sommeil
Les instants
Traduction et Mémoire Poetique

TRANSLATIONS (ITALIAN TO FRENCH)
Tristan, Nanni Balestrini
La Divine comédie, Dante Alighieri
Cinecittá, Federico Fellini
Tout au bout de la mer, Lalla Romano
Le Prince, Machiavel

BOOKS IN ENGLISH
The Translation Begins

ABOUT THE AUTHOR

Born in Besançon, France in 1936, Jacqueline Risset has published many books of poetry as well as literary essays. She was one of the editors of *Tel Quel*, and is well-known for her translations of Dante's *Commedia* (1985-90, fifth edition 2006). Her most recent book is *Traduction et mémoire poétique. Dante, Scève, Rimbaud, Proust* which won the Award of the Académie Française in 2007. She teaches French literature and is President of Centro di Studi Italo-francesi at the Università degli Studi di Roma III.

Sleep's Powers was originally published in French under the title *Puissances du Sommeil* by Éditions du Seuil in September 1997.

TRANSLATOR'S ACKNOWLEDGEMENTS

In her literary inquiries into the powers of sleep Risset often quotes passages from other authors, including Eluard, Char, Proust, Kafka, Bataille, Hölderlin, Nietzsche, Pessoa, Sartre, and Valéry. While the final versions of all such passages are my own, whenever possible I consulted standard English translations as an aid and in an effort to maintain consistency.

The Joyce passage from "When the Sense is Sleep" was quoted from the French text Stèle pour James Joyce, Louis Gillet, Marseille 1941. I owe a debt of gratitude to Sean Latham, editor of the *James Joyce Quarterly*, for assuring me that there is no known English version, so that it was fine for me to translate Joyce back into his native tongue. For an alternative version, see page 712 of Ellmann's renowned biography.

Thanks are due to Rosmarie Waldrop for her suggested changes during the early stages, and to Steve Evans for his role as translation consultant. I would also like to thank Anna Moschovakis for her faith in this book, her keen editorial suggestions, and her thoughtful design and production work.

Earlier versions of certain chapters from *Sleep's Powers* were published in *Verse, Eleven Eleven,* and */nor.* Thanks to all the editors, proof-readers, and typesetters involved.

COLOPHON

This first edition of *Sleep's Powers* is limited to 1,000 copies.

This book was designed and typset by Macabea Can Type, with both text and titles set in Optima. The cover was printed using offset and letterpress printing presses by Polyprintdesign, NYC. The interior was printed and bound by McNaughton and Gunn.

Ugly Duckling Presse is a 501(c)(3) nonprofit publisher based in Brooklyn, NY, which specializes in poetry, translation, lost literature, and books by artists. This book is part of UDP's new Dossier Series, which was created in 2008 to expand the formal scope of the Presse. Dossier publications don't share a single genre or form—long poem, lyric essay, criticism, artist book, polemical text—but rather an investigative impulse. For an updated list of new and forthcoming Dossier titles, point your browser to: www.uglyducklingpresse.org/dossier.